How to Interpret the Bible

JAMES M. EFIRD

Library of Congress Cataloging in Publication Data

Efird, James M.
   How to interpret the Bible.

   Bibliography: p.
   1. Bible—Hermeneutics.   I. Title.
BS476.E35   1984   220.6'01   83-49051
ISBN 0-8042-0069-6

© copyright John Knox Press 1984
10 9 8 7 6 5 4 3 2 1
Printed in the United States of America
John Knox Press
Atlanta, Georgia 30365

In honor of my mother
I. Z. Christy Efird
The Best
PROVERBS 31:10-31

Preface

One of the most popular and often quoted of all books is, of course, the Bible. Unfortunately, however, most of what is popularly known about the Bible stems from ideas and interpretations which are less than accurate. The fact that persons are "sincere" in what they believe the Bible teaches does not make their understandings correct. Proper interpretation of the Bible is really very difficult, for the Bible is a collection of sixty-six books, each of which had a beginning in a specific time and place, quite far removed from present culture and thought patterns. To complicate matters even more, these books were written in other languages—Hebrew, Aramaic, and Greek—and the task of translating these original texts into understandable modern English is not an easy process. In spite of its popularity, the book remains something of a mystery to most people. Understood correctly or not, through the years the Bible has been afforded a place of awe and esteem in the lives of many faithful people, the Hebrew Scriptures (what Christians call the Old Testament) for the communities of Judaism and the Old and New Testaments for the different segments of Christianity. Presently there appears to be a growing hunger on the part of faithful people to study the Bible, to learn what it really says, to understand its meaning and message, and to attempt to relate those teachings to present existence.

This book is an attempt to assist the person who is just beginning to learn how to interpret the Bible. People have attempted in numerous ways to approach the biblical writings and to understand them. The first chapter of this book will examine some of these approaches and attempt to point out strengths and weaknesses of each one. Also suggested will be an approach which will assist the serious student of the Bible in understanding what these texts said *originally*. It is the thesis of this presentation that the heart of biblical study should lie in an attempt to understand what the texts meant as they were originally written by a specific person (or group), directed toward a specific group of persons, in a specific setting, to speak to the needs of those people in that setting. In short, what did the texts originally mean? Unless that question is answered and the teachings of the texts understood as originally intended, modern persons have no possible way to apply correctly the teachings of these texts to modern situations. Some type of safeguard must be built into the process of interpreting the Bible and making it relevant for today's world. Otherwise anyone can argue that any idea, no matter how wrong or farfetched, is "biblical." Unfortunately, too many such interpretations have already been seriously set out and vigorously defended. To repeat, however, sincerity is no guarantee of right.

The suggestions which are made at the end of the first chapter for approaching the biblical texts with a view toward understanding them properly will be specifically applied in the succeeding chapters. These chapters will be arranged basically around the types of literature found in the biblical collection. At the conclusion of each chapter will be a suggested bibliography to facilitate further study by the student.

As one can readily ascertain, this book is not an end in itself but only a first step in assisting persons to learn how to approach the Bible properly and, therefore, to be able to interpret it properly. Other books will greatly assist the student in further study of individual books and in learning more about the methods which are sometimes used by biblical scholars. Two such books will be of significant assistance for the beginning student, and interestingly enough, both are from John Knox Press. The one which is recommended for use with this book and which emphasizes the biblical materials *per se* is by this author, James M. Efird, *These Things Are Written: An Introduction to the Religious Ideas of the Bible*. The second which presents technical methods clearly and which is directed toward helping the student of the Bible understand the text is by John H. Hayes and

Carl R. Holladay, *Biblical Exegesis: A Beginner's Handbook.* These three sources can serve as a guide to proper interpretation and thus to deeper understanding of the biblical materials.

A final chapter will attempt very briefly to suggest ways in which biblical teachings may be applied to modern society and individual lives. This topic deserves a book in itself, for it is not really an easy matter to know how or when to apply these ancient teachings to modern times. If the ancient teachings are to have any meaning other than as curiosities from the past, however, the task of application must be addressed. This book will concentrate, though, on how to interpret the Bible because unless the Bible is properly understood and interpreted *first,* there can be no real application of these teachings. If the teachings are misunderstood, whatever application is made will be incorrect. Far too many misunderstandings of biblical materials are presently at large, and some of them have caused serious problems for people individually and society in general. Wild theories and ideas have been espoused in the name of "the Bible." Proper understanding will eliminate much of this type of misinformation and misapplication. The text must be allowed to say what it says. Whether one agrees immediately with the meaning is really irrelevant, for if one picks and chooses what one agrees with, or if one forces the texts to say what one already believes, the Bible becomes only a tool in the hands of human beings who wish to use the authority and reverence afforded it to impose their own ideas upon others. Proper understanding of the biblical materials is exceedingly important.

I would like to thank the good people at the John Knox Press for their support in allowing this book to be presented and for their assistance in seeing it through to completion. Many church groups, introductory student classes, and ministerial gatherings have also been kind and patient enough to participate in biblical studies with me, and from them I have learned much about what has helped them to understand the Bible better. Thanks are especially in order for the support, encouragement, and assistance of these people through the years. It is for such groups that this book is written with the hope that the Bible can be properly understood. Thanks must also be given once again to my dear wife, Vivian, who has typed both the rough and final copies of this manuscript (as she has all my other efforts) and whose encouragement has made possible the completion of the task.

Finally, a word of appreciation must be given to the one to whom this book is dedicated, my mother. Through many years she has been a constant source of encouragement and assistance. I can remember from my younger days how she would ponder over some biblical passage and say that she understood what the verse said but she was more interested in what it meant; that was the difficult question. Her longing to see the biblical materials interpreted properly has obviously been passed along to me. She is a great lady, and to her this book is lovingly dedicated.

James M. Efird

Contents

I.   Introduction   1

II.   How to Interpret the Torah   19

III.   How to Interpret Historical Books   36

IV.   How to Interpret the Prophets   47

V.   How to Interpret Wisdom   61

VI.   How to Interpret Apocalyptic Literature   74

VII.   How to Interpret the Gospels   90

VIII.   How to Interpret Letters   108

IX.   Conclusion   122

Additional Suggestions for Further Study   131

I

Introduction

The question of how to interpret the Bible properly is of importance to many persons. For the student of history, especially of Western culture, learning what the Bible says and means is of some significance because of the influence the interpretation of the Bible has had on the course of human history. For example, wars have been fought over issues arising out of the interpretation of the Bible. Even some modern political policies are influenced and advocated because of certain understandings of what the Bible says. What part human understandings about the Bible have played in the march of history is of significant import, but even more relevant is the investigation into whether these "forces" were set into motion by proper or improper interpretations of the biblical materials. To understand whether these writings were interpreted properly is, therefore, of value in assessing the movement of history and the impetus which directed that history.

Another aspect of understanding how the interpretation of the Bible has influenced the overall course of history is in learning how biblical interpretations have either assisted or impeded progress in certain areas of society. The investigation into the ways the roles of the Jewish and Christian traditions have modified, changed, or hindered the development of such matters as law, or education, or care of the sick, aged, or orphaned, etc., can be interesting and enlightening indeed. Such research frequently reveals much in which those who are faithful to these traditions can take pride, but also there are times in history which produce painful reminders that even faithful people can make serious mistakes. Usually these mistakes have come from some misinterpretation of the Bible or of some parts of it.

As significant and interesting as a simple historical study may be with regard to proper interpretation of the Bible, an even more important dimension must be considered. This dimension involves those persons who believe that the biblical writings are not simply historical curiosities from the past which have exercised tremendous influence in Western culture (whether rightly or wrongly) but who believe that in the books of the Bible one finds the revelation of God to the world. These people also believe that this revelation contains authoritative teachings concerning the relationship of human beings with God. For these people the task of understanding the Bible properly becomes a matter of much more significance than a simple historical investigation.

Many ecclesiastical bodies have affirmed, for example, that the Bible is a collection of writings which contains "the only infallible rule of faith and practice." If one assumes that this statement is true, it becomes a matter of infinite importance to understand and interpret the Bible properly. In certain traditions the individual believer is urged to read and to study the Bible so that faith can be increased, commitment strengthened, and God's revelation increased in the world.

Unfortunately, however, one of the greatest of the misunderstandings which have been associated with the Bible (and there are many) is that the Bible is a simple book which anyone, anywhere can simply pick up, read, and understand. That idea is, of course, wrong, but it is a misconception which persists and lies at the base of many wild theories and ideas which have been championed and for which biblical authority has been claimed. Some of these will be discussed in the course of this book. It should be obvious, however, that a collection of sixty-six individual books which were written from 1850–2500 years ago (and some of which may contain traditions from as long ago as 3500 years), which arose from cultures with various thought patterns much different from ours, which were written in different languages and in different literary genres just may require some effort on the part of twentieth-century interpreters to understand properly. It may also be that some assistance could be required with regard to background, etc., to facilitate correct understanding of these ancient books.

If persons do believe that these books contain God's revelation to the world, it is a serious matter to ensure that these documents are interpreted properly. And the consequences can be disastrous if instead of listening to what these books really say, one simply finds within these books what one wishes to find. In such an instance the interpreter is *not* receiving God's revelation but rather simply reading into and therefore out of the texts one's own opinions. The biblical books may as well not exist if such is the case.

It is exceedingly important, therefore to learn how to interpret these writings correctly, to learn what they mean, not only what they say. The search for that meaning can be rewarding, exhilarating, and even fun. In order to set the stage for the suggestions to be presented here concerning proper methods and approaches to use in interpreting the biblical books, it is perhaps wise to review briefly some of the ways people are approaching these documents today. Space will not allow for an exhaustive listing of all approaches, and some of the positions will by necessity be somewhat caricatured, but the strengths and weaknesses of each position should be pointed out especially to the beginning biblical interpreter.

The Plenary Proof-text Method

Some have argued that the books of the Bible are "fully" inspired (thus the word "plenary") by the Spirit of God. Being so inspired, every sentence, every phrase, every word is understood to be charged with theological meaning and suitable for direction in all aspects of the life of the religious person. Not one word is to be lost or overlooked for its intended revelation of God's word to the world. Such an understanding has led some to view individual verses or even pieces of verses as containing absolute doctrine and dogma. Various bits and pieces of text have then been used to develop or support certain theological ideas and positions not really taught in the larger context of the book.

Such an attitude can be commendable in that proponents of this method acknowledge the inspired nature of these documents and their importance for the lives of those faithful persons who look toward these books for direction in their thinking about God and in their day-to-day behavior. The Bible is taken seriously and is held in highest esteem by advocates of such a position.

The danger of this type of understanding is that it places too much importance on *all* components of the biblical materials, disallowing any real development in the religious understandings and teachings contained in the biblical material. Too much is made of small portions of the text ripped apart from their larger contexts. Words, even the words of the Bible, have no real meaning, however, apart from larger contexts. To cite a text by itself can be greatly misleading if not downright wrong. For example, in Genesis 3:5 one can read the words, "you will be like God." If the interpreter examines this sentence in its context, it becomes clear that the meaning of the saying is an attempt to deceive, a cruel hoax. Some have understood this passage in an entirely different way from its intended and plain meaning in the original context, interpreting it to imply that human beings can become gods! This is certainly not the intent of this saying, as most people instantly recognize when they read the larger context.

Numerous groups are responsible for perpetuating this form of biblical interpretation. People who fall into this mode range all the way from persons who are very sincere but know no other approach to some powerful theologians who sometimes like to cite verses or pieces of verses to build theological systems. Perhaps one of the most persistent offenders at this point is the preaching clergy. Faced with having to prepare a sermon (sometimes two) for every Sunday and being confronted with numerous issues and problems in the church, many preachers resort to lifting texts out of context or to fanciful interpretations of phrases in any given verse in order to preach topically without having to do serious study of the biblical material per se. This is not to imply that these people are not serious, well-meaning, and sincere in their admiration and devotion to the Scriptures. Most certainly are, but serious, well-meaning, and sincere are not guarantees of correct interpretation. The use of the Bible to support and defend theological ideas and modes of thought and behavior which clearly are not what the biblical writers intended simply distorts the true meaning and intention of the texts. Some of the many outlandish understandings will be addressed specifically in the course of the development of this discussion.

The Literal Approach

Another group which holds that each and every word or phrase of the Bible is inspired has argued that in order to understand the message from God contained in the biblical books, one must interpret all the parts literally. As with the proof-text method these persons hold that all verses and units, even short phrases, are to be understood as containing authoritative doctrine. Many persons in this category boast that they take the Bible "literally." The truth is, however, that no one really does this. What many persons mean by such a statement is that they believe in the inerrancy or the infallibility of the Bible. Their understanding is that the Bible (at least the original documents) had no errors whatsoever, and that all parts of the writings are absolutely literally true, not only religiously but *in historical and scientific detail also*.

Such an approach often causes interesting responses to troubling questions. If the two creation accounts differ, for example, they must describe two parts of the same event—even if the "literal" details do not match. If in the Synoptic Gospels (i.e., Matthew, Mark, and Luke), Jesus cleanses the temple at the beginning of the week of his death, and if in John's Gospel, Jesus cleanses the temple at the very beginning of his ministry (three years before his death), then Jesus must have cleansed the temple twice. The fact that these accounts are almost certainly two versions of the same story is irrelevant to such persons. So is the observation that the biblical writers do not really seem to be obsessed (as some modern interpreters are) with the absolute historical validity of every statement in every story. For example, just as there are two different accounts of creation, so there are also two accounts of the flood. In one Noah was commanded to take one pair of each animal aboard the ark (cf. Gen. 6:19–20.), and in the other he was told to take seven pairs of clean animals and one pair of unclean animals (cf. Gen. 7:2–3.). Further, Mark 1:2 tells the reader that the Scripture to be quoted is from Isaiah. Upon examination, however, it emerges that the quotation is composed from Malachi and Exodus in addition to Isaiah. Mark 2:26 states that Abiathar was high priest when David and his men ate the "bread of the Presence," but 1 Samuel 21:1 states that Ahimelech was high priest then. Such "errors" or inconsistencies should not really concern interpreters of the biblical books because absolute specificity was not an obsession with the writers of these documents. Much more important issues were at stake.

A "literalistic" approach also ignores the plain fact that many different types of literature are included among the biblical writings. Some types of literature were never intended to be taken literally, poetry to cite only one example. The famous saying, "My love is like a red, red rose," loses all its beauty when subjected to analysis from the perspective of absolute literalism. The Bible is filled with poetry and many other types of literature as well—sagas, theological histories, short stories, wisdom sayings, apocalyptic images, to cite only a few (they will be defined later)—which were not intended to be understood literally.

Interestingly enough many persons who claim to be literalists really are not. For example, when asked about such figures as the beast in Revelation 13, they respond, "Oh, the beast stands for . . . ," and they begin to make an analogy to some modern person or institution. Such an interpretation is, then, no longer a "literal" one. A literal understanding would mean that the beast *is* a beast, no more and no less.

Understanding what kind of literary type one is studying in a biblical book or passage is very important, so that the interpreter will know whether the passage was intended to be taken literally or figuratively. One simply cannot be a "literalist" in interpreting the Bible, for many texts themselves demonstrate that this approach is not helpful in understanding the message of the biblical passage and that the biblical writers themselves did not understand them in such a way.

The Existentialist Approach

Other persons who interpret the Bible believe that the most important goal which can be achieved from the study of that book constitutes the finding of directions and teachings which can be applied to individual and societal problems today. The question asked by these persons when they approach the biblical materials is: what does this text say "to me"? The obvious advantage of this approach is that such persons seriously believe they can find in the biblical materials ideas, rules for living, philosophies, and the like, which are relevant to present human existence. The Bible is not simply a book of antiquity, but it can speak powerfully to people in any age.

Unfortunately, however, many advocates of this position allow too much leeway to their own "feelings" and quite frequently read their own ideas and philosophies "into" and then "out of" the biblical texts. In such a procedure the text too often becomes only a mirror reflecting the image of the one looking into the documents. Only those parts of the biblical writings which appear relevant "to me" are considered valuable, and the remaining portions are ignored if not rejected. Such an approach falls prey in some respects to the same criticism as the "proof-text" method in that the original settings and meanings of the writings are frequently ignored.

Some advocates of this position also have a tendency to ignore teachings which do not appeal to the interpreter at some particular moment since those texts do not presently speak "to me." Many people also dismiss or disregard some of the more difficult passages which do not seem at first glance to have any relevance to modern society or culture. In short, this method of approach tends to be highly subjective, and quite frequently the meaning and relevance of the text is directly related to one's "feelings" at any given moment. The most dangerous aspect of this approach is the attitude of some interpreters who assume that any portions of the biblical materials which teach ideas or philosophies with which the interpreter disagrees can be dismissed.

The Literary Approach

In recent years certain groups have begun to analyze the biblical writings from the standpoint of literary criticism, i.e., they understand the Bible as a collection of literary creations which must be interpreted according to the conventions of the various literary genres. It is, of course, true that the biblical books have been understood to be literary creations for centuries. With this recent literary approach, however, persons come to these materials armed with the canons of literary criticism as that discipline is practiced currently by literary critics.

Naturally, much merit can be found in such an approach, for it is obviously true that these books are literary creations, wholistic units, and should be understood as such when interpreted. This approach escapes the pitfalls of the "proof-text" method which looks too often only at bits and pieces of the materials and also of the existentialist approach which only accepts as valid those passages which speak "to me." The strength of this method lies in its understanding of the biblical materials as literary units and the understanding that there are many different types of literature. Understanding how a particular literary form came into being, the presuppositions and intentions of persons who wrote in these forms, and the message usually conveyed by these literary units assist an interpreter tremendously in discovering the real intent and meaning of the materials.

Unfortunately, many of those persons who have advocated such an approach have been trained in modern methods of analyzing sophisticated literature. These modern literary critics have applied the guidelines of their discipline to the more ancient and less sophisticated biblical materials. Quite frequently, therefore, far too much is read into and then out of the ancient documents than is really there. It is one thing to find hidden meanings and symbolism in modern writings; it is another to read ideas not intended by the authors into the biblical materials. Interestingly enough, even some contemporary writers make the same negative observations about modern literary analysts and critics!

The Psychological/Sociological Approach

In some circles it has become popular to subject the biblical accounts and the characters depicted in those accounts to the interpretative canons of modern psychological and sociological theories. Not so long ago it was considered quite acceptable to psychoanalyze such biblical characters as Moses or the prophets (Jeremiah and Ezekiel were favorites here) or Jesus and his disciples or Paul, etc., so that one could understand the religious ideas of the Bible in modern psychological categories. By so doing, it was argued, the interpreter could gain insight into the dynamics of human understanding with regard to religious matters so that religious teachings common to the biblical writings and other religious communities and philosophies might be clearly discerned. The emphasis here is upon common denominators among the various religious traditions of the world as these relate to the psychological makeup of human beings. Much was made of the parallel teachings; the uniqueness of the biblical writings was sometimes ignored.

Another dimension of the emphasis upon the psychological approach has been the tendency for some interpreters (preachers probably again being the worst offenders) to "create" thoughts and feelings for the persons depicted in biblical accounts. This has been labeled by some as "psychologizing." The most popular form of this is the reading into the minds of the biblical characters what they "must have thought" in this or that situation and setting. Such a method may at points suggest valid ideas and insights, but this method too runs the risk of allowing the interpreter to project into the text the interpreter's own ideas and feelings, and thus to make the interpreter's thoughts as authoritative as the sacred text itself.

In addition to psychological analyses of the biblical writers and personalities there has been more recently a decided shift toward an emphasis on sociological investigation to shed light on the biblical accounts. Practices and tendencies in other sociological settings which could be considered similar to biblical movements have been examined so that biblical practices and movements can be explained or enlightened by drawing parallels. The idea is that if, sociologically speaking, the interpreter can locate parallels between the events or behavior of some other culture which seems to give insight into similar events and behavior in the biblical materials, this would explain the reasons for the emergence of such events and behavior among the biblical peoples. It would, further, give insight into the proper interpretation of these items.

While information which may be gleaned about the development of certain sociological phenomena in various cultures can be of value in understanding some of the biblical texts, this approach also has a tendency to emphasize a "common denominator" relationship between other cultures and the biblical settings. This can be helpful in some instances, but it runs the risk of failing to see the uniqueness which may be present in each of the cultures! There have been instances when even twentieth-century investigations of twentieth-century tribes or peoples have been used to explain events and movements which occurred more than 3000 years ago.

Both of these areas of research can add much to one's understanding of the religious ideas of the communities and persons which produced the various biblical books. Once more, however, such attempts have become all too frequently a means whereby a great deal has been read into the materials which may not be there. Attempting to psychoanalyze the biblical writers or characters, for example, often becomes a game whereby interpreters project their own psychological ideas into and onto these materials with the result that they find only a reflection of their own ideas and feelings. Likewise, various attempts to understand certain of the significant movements within the biblical traditions against the backdrop of parallel developments in other societies (some of which are much later, centuries in fact) frequently force categories and traditions and interpretations upon the biblical materials that may not have been originally intended and which may be misleading in the interpretative process.

The Historical-Critical Approach

The historical-critical method is the keystone of modern academic study of the Bible. This approach subjects the biblical materials to the same kinds of searching analysis applied with the same method and vigor which are used on any other document of the past. The task of this endeavor is to discover as best one can the "who, what, where, when, and why" of these ancient writings. (Who wrote what? where? when? why? to whom?) The obvious strength of such an approach rests in its emphasis on uncovering and discovering the original setting and original meaning of these documents. Needless to say, since this is the basic approach of the academic community, this approach with its many facets and various methodological theories tends to be quite analytical and often leads to speculative conjectures concerning the materials and their meaning.

For the interpretation of any text, in order to understand its meaning, one must examine that text in its own historical setting.

This means that such an approach as the historical-critical one outlined here must be a part of the proper interpretation of biblical texts. The problem too often with the modern academic community has been that its members have become far too detached from the text and have failed to understand the biblical books as products of a faith community for a faith community. Far too often the academic enterprise has become an end in itself, sometimes playing games with the text, rather than a means of facilitating proper interpretation. Several comments by recent writers illustrate the point being made.

Walter Wink, in *The Bible in Human Transformation: Toward a New Paradigm for Biblical Study* (Philadelphia: Fortress Press, 1973), begins with a blast: "Historical biblical criticism is bankrupt" (p. 1). Professor Wink's criticism of this method is not without precedent, but the significance of his comments is enhanced when one learns that he is himself a biblical scholar. Some of his comments, therefore, deserve serious attention. He declares:

> We will see . . . that the historical critical method had a vested interest in undermining the Bible's authority, that it operated as a background ideology for the demystification of religious tradition, that it required functional atheism for its practice,. . . .
> The historical critical method has reduced the Bible to a dead letter. Our obeisance to technique has left the Bible sterile and ourselves empty (pp. 3–4).

Wink argues that the liberal church in its early days used historical-critical research as its weapon against rigid orthodoxy, and as liberal ideology began to be successful, the guild of biblical scholars gradually became the "community of reference and accountability" for the interpretation of the Bible rather than the church community. "For scholarship it was disastrous because the questions asked the texts were seldom ones on which human lives hinged, but those most likely to win a hearing from the guild" (p. 10). He continues:

> To say that biblical criticism has now, like revivalism, become bankrupt, is simply to summarize the entire discussion to this point. It was based on an inadequate method, married to a false objectivism, subjected to uncontrolled technologism, separated from a vital

community, and has outlived its usefulness as presently practiced. Whether or not it has any future at all depends on its adaptability to a radically altered situation (p. 15).

Another comment along the same lines appeared rather recently. "Professional scholars who write about the Bible are tempted to consider it a mother lode for mining a scholarly living, . . . " according to James A. Fischer in *How to Read the Bible* (Englewood Cliffs, N. J.: Prentice-Hall, Inc., 1982, p. ix).

These comments, especially those by Professor Wink, may well be somewhat overstated. It is true, unfortunately, that the faith community which looks to the biblical writings with more than simple historical curiosity usually does not have the same questions and concerns as the scholarly guild. This difference of emphasis and outlook has led to an adversarial relationship at times between the two groups. The arrogance of some in the academic community has produced very negative feelings among those in the faith community toward scholarly endeavors; this is tragic but probably deserved. Conversely, many in the faith community have reacted with equal disdain toward academic investigation and study of the biblical books. The caution here, as with most of the other approaches, must be not to allow some misunderstandings or wrong interpretations or the like to blind the interpreter's eyes to the positive elements in the method. The abuse of the method by some should not deter one from the positive uses of the approach.

To cite Professor Wink once again: "The model for students should be not the biblical scholar, but the biblical interpreter—a person competent to help any group of people understand the impact of the Bible in human transformation" (p. 77). The true biblical interpreter must not only understand what the Bible *says* but must also have a similar "faith stance" with the biblical communities in order to understand what these books really *mean*. How can these two dimensions be united in such a way as to produce proper and correct biblical interpretation? The following discussion is an attempt to demonstrate how this may be done.

A Suggested Method for Interpreting the Bible

The reader may well wonder just what type of method may still be available for use after having examined several of the various approaches and learning that each one has its shortcomings and weaknesses. Not only does each have weaknesses but the primary weakness of each one is that the individual interpreter may manipulate the method so as to find in the text what one wishes to find! The truth is that no one approach can guarantee correct interpretation or absolutely guard against misunderstandings and misinterpretations, honest or otherwise. In fact, probably no ironclad method exists which can protect persons from misinterpretations of the Scriptures no matter how hard one might try to find such an approach. What will be suggested here is an approach to interpreting the Scriptures which, if followed carefully, will help one to understand the biblical books better and can definitely guard against outlandish and distorted interpretations.

The approach to be proposed here can be designated *eclectic*, utilizing the strengths of each of the methods but guarding against the abuses and/or extremes sometimes perpetrated by overzealous advocates of one single position. Any approach to interpretation, however, must have a focus, a base, a foundation stone upon which the interpretative structure may be built. The suggested *base* for proper biblical interpretation presented here must lie in the answer to this question: *what did these books mean originally?* This appears to be the one absolutely essential element in proper biblical interpretation. To discover the answer to that question several others must also be asked. What do the texts say? How were they understood by those who wrote them? How did those people for whom the books were originally intended understand them? The foundation stone for interpreting the Bible properly, then, is the discovery of the original meaning. If this be true, then some form of the historical-critical method must be a basic part of this process. Supposedly the aim and goal of that method is precisely to recover the original meaning of the documents. Naturally a part of the investigation to discover the original meaning will also include some analysis of the sociological settings for the individual writings both in the larger milieu of the ancient world and in the specific setting of the people who produced those books and to whom they were directed. Further, if anything can be known about the psychological dimensions involved in those times, that too would add significantly to understanding the texts.

While some form of the historical-critical method of investigation, supplemented by sociological and psychological studies, must therefore lie at the heart of proper biblical interpretation, yet another of the procedures must be considered especially by persons who are beginners at this art. (Proper and correct interpretation of any document is really an art.) This very important element which greatly augments the other approaches lies in the literary nature of the texts. Each of the biblical writings was composed as a literary unit (or as part of a larger literary unit) to be read, studied, and understood in its entirety, not subjected to piecemeal analysis. These larger literary units must be recognized and understood if proper interpretation is to take place, for there are different types of literature found among the biblical writings. It is well known that one simply does not interpret every type of literature in the same way. Some types, for example, were never intended to be understood literally. There are, for example, many poetic passages among the biblical materials, and most school children know that poetry is not to be understood in a wooden literalistic way. To interpret poetry correctly, interpreters must allow the poet "poetic license," and this courtesy must be afforded to the ancient poets as well as their modern counterparts. One surely does not really believe that the biblical poet actually thought that mountains could sing or that trees had hands to clap (cf. Isa. 55:12). In dealing with the biblical materials smaller literary units (such as poetry) are found in the larger literary compositions. This means that at times the biblical interpreter will be dealing with mixtures of literary types. Recognizing such literary units, either large or small, and understanding how they were intended to be understood greatly enhances the interpretative process.

After the interpreter has examined a book (or group of books) from the perspective and background of its historical-critical, sociological, psychological, and literary components, understanding the original meaning of the text is much more possible than if one comes to the text already presupposing what is there and yet ignorant of vital information necessary to interpret the text properly. If the interpreter approaches the text as objectively as possible (realizing that no one can be totally objective), using the guidelines proposed here, the meaning of the biblical texts begins to become clear. Sometimes surprises are in store because many texts simply do not mean what they have been popularly assumed to mean. The question which arises at this point is does this text and its meaning have any relevance for life either individually or collectively today? How can one transfer the ideas, principles, and meaning of the ancient documents into the present? This is the second step in the interpretative process, determining if there is any present relevance to the ancient meanings.

If one believes that the Bible is God's revelation to humankind and one is a member of the faith community, the answer to that question has to be answered in the affirmative. Yet the process of making a transition from the biblical text to a modern setting can be quite tricky. What happens, unfortunately, all too often is that a "leap" is made from the Bible to a supposed modern parallel which just happens to be a pet idea of the interpreter. Quite frequently the biblical teaching under consideration just happens to agree exactly with the interpreter's position! At this point one is back to reading into the texts what one wishes to find there.

For example, presently many good and conscientious persons intensely long for world peace. This is a noble ideal, worthy of commitment and effort. Many of those who are involved in this movement use biblical texts to support their cause. These people argue for nuclear disarmament and even unilateral disarmament. They assume that since the biblical materials contain many references to "peace" that the writers intended and understood peace in exactly the same way as that concept is being championed today. Many argue that "peace" occurs when active hostilities cease. "Peace" as used by the writers of the biblical books, however, means much more than that. The word means something like "total well-being," a concept that far exceeds a simple cessation of hostilities. On the other hand, others have argued that since the Bible (in some sections) endorses the concept of "Holy War" that this opens the door for "wars of liberation" or "just wars" or even wars to extend "the faith."

Each of these groups fails, however, to take into account the larger *overall* meaning of the biblical writings, the principles espoused in those writings, and the caution that one must be very careful not to read modern theories and ideas back into the ancient texts. The texts must be understood first as they were originally written.

Any cultural ideas or motifs must be recognized. Then, one finds in these texts underlying *principles* or *truth* which may be applied in modern settings, if these settings are historically or otherwise analogous to the original setting. These guidelines can guard against the "too superficial" application of a biblical teaching to a modern setting which is not really addressed by that teaching. Again modern interpreters must be extremely cautious not to read their own ideas and philosophies into the biblical texts and then claim divine authority for them!

Before there can be any modern application, however, the fundamental question must be resolved: what did these texts originally say *and mean?* The remainder of this book is presented in the hope that by demonstrating the use of the guidelines suggested, the person who wishes to learn how to interpret the Bible properly will find some beginning insights and principles and a method for approaching the texts. The primary emphasis here will be upon the insights of the literary method because that approach has been found by this writer to be the most helpful among persons who are just beginning to learn how to take biblical interpretation seriously. The literary segments of the biblical materials which will be examined are the Torah, the historical books, the prophetic materials, the wisdom writings, and apocalyptic materials, the Gospels, and letters. Finally, a summary will offer some suggestions for ways in which the meanings of the biblical materials may be applied to present situations. The emphasis of this study, however, is upon introducing the beginning student to a method by which the original meanings of the biblical texts can be ascertained today.

Suggestions for Further Study

Achtemeier, Paul J. *The Inspiration of Scripture: Problems and Proposals.* Philadelphia: Westminster Press, 1980.

Fischer, James A. *How to Read the Bible.* Englewood Cliffs, N. J.: Prentice-Hall, Inc., 1982.

Greenspahn, Frederick E., (ed.). *Scripture in the Jewish and Christian Traditions: Authority, Interpretation, Relevance.* Nashville: Abingdon Press, 1982.

Grollenberg, Lucas H. *Bible Study for the 21st Century*, translated by John E. Steely. Wilmington, N.C.: Consortium Books, 1976.

Ricoeur, Paul. *Essays on Biblical Interpretation*. Philadelphia: Fortress Press, 1980.

Sire, James W. *Scripture Twisting: 20 Ways the Cults Misread the Bible*. Downer's Grove, Ill.: Inter-Varsity Press, 1980.

Smart, James D. *The Interpretation of Scripture*. Philadelphia: Westminster Press, 1961.

Stacey, Walter David. *Interpreting the Bible*. New York: Hawthorn Books, 1977.

———. *Groundwork of Biblical Studies*. Minneapolis: Augsburg Press, 1982.

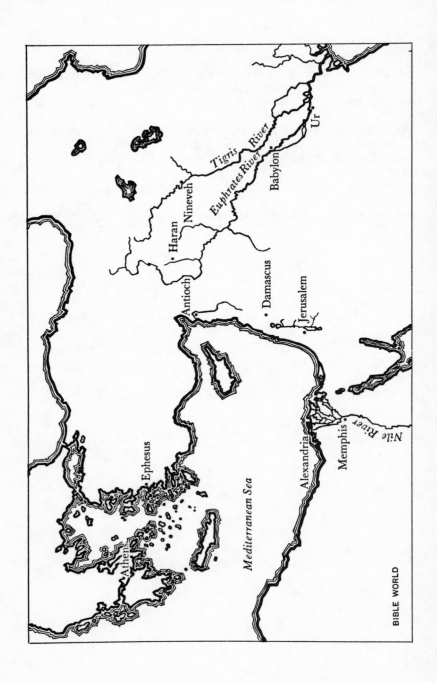

BIBLE WORLD

II

How to Interpret
the Torah

The Torah or Pentateuch (Genesis, Exodus, Leviticus, Numbers, Deuteronomy) was the first section of the Hebrew Scriptures to be canonized, i.e., accepted as authoritative for the life of the religious community. Most scholars believe that this collection of books was edited into the form in which it now exists by about 400–350 B.C. These books came to be known as the "Books of Moses" primarily because Moses is the central figure in the basic story which the writings relate. Later this designation came to be understood as referring to Moses as the author of the books, but as more recent scholarship has rather adequately demonstrated this thesis simply cannot be sustained.

The process by which the traditions of the Hebrew people came to be contained as they are in the books of the Torah is quite complicated. Scholars argue almost constantly about various aspects of the entire process, and it must be admitted that much of the theorizing is precisely that. Careful study of the documents themselves, however, reveals certain characteristics, methodology, and literary types which give some evidence of the process. The following brief survey is given only to suggest some broad outlines and background for understanding that process.

The Documentary Hypothesis

Most scholars agree that in the ancient background of the Hebrew people were many tribes and peoples, each with its own history and traditions, which finally came together after the Exodus event to form the nation, Israel. Many of these diverse traditions had been remembered and passed along orally from generation to generation until they were blended together into larger blocks of material, some of which remained oral and some of which had begun to be written down. Somewhere in the process someone or someones collected certain of these units of tradition together in an attempt to form a coherent history of the people of Israel. The first attempt probably came about 950 B.C. (during the reign of Solomon who encouraged such activity) by a writer or editor usually known as the Yahwist, designated by the letter J because the Hebrew name for God, YHWH, is read as *Jahwe(h)* in German. This "history" made use of various traditions, primarily Judean, and presented the Hebrew people as part of God's larger plan for the world which explains why there was a primitive creation account at its beginning (cf. Gen. 2:4—3:24).

Numerous stylistic, historical, and religious peculiarities characterize the J materials scattered throughout Genesis, Exodus, Numbers, and Joshua. The most famous particularity, however, lies in the idea of the Yahwist that God was known to the Hebrew people from the very beginning of creation as Yahweh. In those days the gods had specific names; Yahweh was the name by which the Hebrew people knew God.

A second attempt to depict Hebrew history originated in Northern Israel sometime after the split of Solomon's kingdom into (Northern) Israel and (Southern) Judah in 922/1 B.C.. This account was probably composed as a parallel version of the Yahwistic history but from the perspective of the northern tribes. The designation for this strand of tradition which was ultimately used in the final composition of the Torah is E, for Elohist. The term Elohist is derived from the generic term for God in Hebrew, *Elohîm*, because in this set of traditions the Hebrew people did not know the name Yahweh for God until the time of Moses and the Exodus. Most of the traditions and stories used in this composition centered in northern sites and personalities. As with the Yahwist traditions, numerous stylistic, historical, and religious peculiarities are found in E.

The latest of the blocks of tradition which must be noted in dealing with the Torah is called P because these materials are heavily weighted toward matters with which priests are concerned. Proper rituals and proper keeping of the ancient commands are fundamental to this strand. In fact, most scholars are agreed that the P traditions derived from a Priestly group which was primarily responsible for editing the Torah in essentially its present form. Again there are certain characteristics and emphases of this strand of traditions as there were with both J and E.

From these three strands of traditions primarily, the Priestly group (mentioned above) wove together and structured a history of the Hebrew people from their primitive beginnings and set that history within the larger context of world history and God's intentions for them and for the world. How these three strands originated, developed, and were finally edited together is a complicated problem. Scholars cannot reach a unified consensus as to the exact details of how all this developed. It is not our task here to rehearse all the problems or to reach definitive conclusions but simply to give broad guidelines for foundational purposes. Suffice it to say that sometime during and after the Exile of the Judean people in Babylon (587–538 B.C.) these strands of tradition were brought together and formed a "Priestly" history of the Hebrew people from the creation through the settlement of the tribes in the land of Canaan. This history probably contained what we now know as Genesis, Exodus, Leviticus, Numbers, and Joshua.

Deuteronomic History

At this point we must digress a bit from our more narrow investigation of the Torah and examine another literary phenomenon which also came to fruition in the exilic and post-exilic periods. A group of people, perhaps from a prophetic lineage, put together another "history" of the Hebrew people which began with Moses and the Exodus, outlined the history of the nation through its earliest times, described the rise of the monarchy in Israel, the establishment of the

United Kingdom, and then traced the fortunes of the divided nations of Israel and Judah until their downfalls. The books of Deuteronomy, Judges, Samuel, and Kings constituted this "history." Incorporated into these books were traditions and excerpts from many other sources (other than J, E, P) available at that time. Since the history, known as the Deuteronomistic or Deuteronomic history, concludes in the midst of the Exile (561 B.C.), many scholars believe that it was composed about that time.

Several characteristics were emphasized in this literary work. Two motifs are most important to keep in mind in order to understand the material as it now stands. First is a decided emphasis on the idea of covenant. This is not to imply that this motif is not also found in the Priestly history, but whereas the covenant in the Priestly history involves the land and God's promise concerning the land, the covenant in the Deuteronomic history is centered in the nation and the king, especially the covenant with David and his descendants to rule over Judah.

The second emphasis of the Deuteronomic history involves a certain theological understanding closely related to the idea of covenant. That idea revolves around the belief that if a nation or people is loyal to Yahweh and keeps Yahweh's commands, then that group will be blessed and will prosper. If it does not, then judgment will surely come upon them. The student will find numerous examples of this thinking throughout the books of Deuteronomy, Judges, Samuel, and Kings. The book of Judges in particular exhibits this theological understanding of history by arranging the traditions in the following sequence: apostasy—judgment—repentance—deliverance. The people disobey Yahweh; Yahweh sends a judgment or punishment upon them; the people cry out and repent; Yahweh delivers them from the oppression. After this, there is calm for a period of time.

To state unequivocally exactly what the purpose was in compiling the Deuteronomic history would be to exceed the bounds of our knowledge. Numerous theories have, nevertheless, been suggested. The one which seems to make the most logical sense is that the Deuteronomic history was written to explain to the Judean people in Exile in Babylonia why they were there (and why their northern kin were no longer in existence at all) and also to give them hope. If God's people repent after judgment, God can restore them and renew the covenant with them again. This message would have brought great comfort to the community in Exile.

The Pentateuch

During the Exile and afterward, therefore, these two "histories" of the Hebrews were prepared, each compiled to speak not only to the ancient history of the people but to their present concerns as well. Each was composed of various sources and strands of tradition put together to illustrate certain ideas and concerns of the two groups (i.e., the Priestly and the Deuteronomic). At this stage neither of these was considered "Scripture" though each was probably considered "special" with regard to the history and religion of the Hebrew people. Sometime between the Exile and about 400 B.C., however, certain persons obviously took the first parts of the Priestly history and the first part of the Deuteronomic history and combined these together into basically what we know today as the Torah or Pentateuch. Exactly why this was done cannot be known, but it appears obvious that the figure of Moses and the event of the Exodus were the keys to this process. The people of God was established in the Exodus event and the covenant made between Yahweh and Israel. Since what is now the book of Joshua contained materials after Moses, this segment of the Priestly history was interchanged with the book of Deuteronomy which was the first segment of the Deuteronomic history. The story of the death of Moses which was probably at the end of what is now called Numbers was moved to the end of Deuteronomy to conclude this collection. (What happened to the book of Joshua will be discussed later.)

This literary collection called the Torah then centered on Moses, the Exodus, Yahweh's covenant with the people, and the rules for how to be Yahweh's people. What is known now as the book of Genesis served as an introduction to Moses and the Exodus and rooted this small group of people in God's plan for the world from the very beginning, i.e., from creation.

It should be obvious to most persons that the Torah is therefore composed of numerous stories and traditions which were passed along for hundreds of years before being put into writing. At each stage of the journey the material was used in new situations as circumstances were altered. Various disciplines have emerged in the study of the Hebrew Scriptures which study these traditions, their origins, transmission, use, and interpretation; these are called form criticism, tradition criticism, and source criticism. It is not the purpose of this book to investigate and explicate these areas of specialization. Other books introduce these very well (cf. especially John Hayes and Carl Holladay, *Biblical Exegesis: A Beginner's Handbook* [Atlanta: John Knox Press, 1983]). Suffice it to say here that while these disciplines are exceedingly helpful in assisting the student in the pursuit of biblical studies, they also tend to be highly speculative in nature, and quite frequently one is hard pressed to find agreement among the proponents of the various approaches. The beginning student should be aware of these methods but for the time being concentrate on the study of the books as literary units and on literary types and motifs as these may be found within the larger works.

Background for the Study of the Torah

The Torah contains the most ancient traditions and stories found in all the biblical writings. Embedded in these larger units of tradition (J, E, P, and D), therefore, are numerous smaller units. These units are not all the same type and do not all serve the same purpose. One of the most common of these units is called the *saga* or legend. Such stories which told of the great heroes and their exploits (such as those dealing with Abraham, Isaac, and Jacob) were used to help the people and the community to link themselves with a distinguished past. Most of these types of stories have some historical kernel of fact within them, but they are so far removed from their origins by the time they were put into written form that it is impossible to be able to say with precision exactly what happened, when, who said what, etc. Preoccupation with such matters, however, is a modern problem; the original composers and hearers of these stories and documents were not primarily concerned with external historical specificity but with the religious meanings which the stories conveyed.

The Hebrews, as most of the cultures and societies of the ancient world, were extremely curious about why things are as they are in this world. What caused the world to be as it is? There was, therefore, a certain literary motif which was utilized by ancient peoples to explain these curious and puzzling phenomena. This device is called *etiology*, explaining *why* some aspect of the world is as it is. This motif may be found within stories or may even be the dominant idea of a particular story. Secular or nonreligious explanations were suggested for such phenomena by some societies, but the Hebrews clothed all such explanations in religious garb. For example, in Genesis 3:14–19 religious explanations are given for such phenomena as why the snake crawls on its belly, why women have pain in childbirth, why people work so hard for so little, etc. The reason for all these problems lies in the disobedience toward God of the first humans, with the clear understanding that such problems are continued and even exaggerated by the continuation of that disobedience of God by humanity. Everything in the Hebrew mind could be explained by reference to religion. There are many etiological stories in the Bible.

Another device the Hebrews used to explain events and ideas with religious interpretations was that of "concretizing" everything in specific historical settings. If, for example, a custom was practiced in Hebrew life and the original reason for that custom had been lost in the misty recesses of the past, a significant event, more recent and well-known, was attached to the practice and these were interpreted together. An excellent example of such a practice is the Passover festival. This ancient rite was practiced by some of the tribes and peoples who ultimately came together to form "Israel." The origins of that custom were either forgotten or ignored; therefore the origin and significance of that practice were transferred to *the* great event, the Exodus from Egypt. In this one can readily see how the Hebrew people used ancient traditions and customs, sometimes blending them together to form ideas and practices with new religious interpretations. One can also begin to understand the tendency toward concretizing ideas and practices by identifying them with specific historical settings.

Another literary type which the ancients used is called "myth." Many persons in modern society who are devoted to the Bible as God's revelation are quite upset and become very defensive when someone suggests that there may be some "myths" in the biblical accounts. There is no need for concern here, however, if one keeps in mind what is meant by the use of that term in biblical settings. The term "myth" in modern settings sometimes suggests something untrue, a fabrication deliberately used to deceive people. Such are not the implications of the word when associated with biblical writings, however. There the word signifies a story told to explain the activities of the god or gods as these activities relate to the world of human existence and experiences. Most stories of this type were told to explain events and activities that human beings were not involved in, such as creation, or if they were, no account of that activity has been left by those persons who may have been involved. Many myths are found among the writings of ancient peoples, but surprisingly enough very few "pure myths" are found in the biblical writings. The reason for this is obviously a result of the Hebrew tendency to concretize such teachings within the bounds of the historical process. The closest one gets to such stories are the creation accounts, the account of the flood, and the story of the confusion of languages at Babel (Genesis 11). Even in these stories, however, the interpreter already finds a tendency to "demythologize" the accounts by linking the stories to history as much as possible. Perhaps a brief examination of the creation stories will assist the beginner in understanding this type approach.

Creation Accounts

Two creation accounts are found in Genesis 1—3. If one reads these accounts with any kind of objectivity at all, it becomes very clear that these two accounts are *quite* different and cannot be understood or explained as supplementary to each other. Why are there two accounts if the purpose is to give a scientific and historical account of how creation took place? The answer to that question is obvious: that was *not* the purpose of the biblical writers. One is reminded that religious matters and ideas were important to the Hebrews, not historical specificity especially when dealing in areas that could not have been observed by humans. Creation obviously was one of these areas!

The first account is found in Genesis 1:1—2:3 and the second in

2:4—3:24. If one examines these stories carefully, it becomes apparent that the second account comes from the J traditions and the first account from the P traditions. The Yahwist, as already noted, compiled his history about 950 B.C. and linked the people of God directly to God's creation and the first human beings. This account is characterized by primitive ideology, the use of anthropomorphisms (the attributing to God of human form) and anthropopathisms (the attributing to God of human feelings), and numerous etiological motifs. Yahweh creates a male human being first, places him in a garden paradise to "keep it and till it," creates animals to assist the man, and finally creates a woman to be his special helper. The humans disobey Yahweh's command, attempting to take God's place (cf. 3:5). For that rebellion they suffer consequences, which explains why certain things are as they are in this world. This story also explains death as the result of human sin. Whether death in this context is to be understood as physical death only is debated, but it seems clear from the story that death means more than simple physical demise which is part of the created order. Real death occurs when humans attempt to usurp God's rightful place as center of their existence, thereby cutting themselves off from the source of real life.

The first account in Genesis 1:1—2:3 is the later of the two, probably composed during the Exile in Babylon (about 550 B.C.). The Babylonians were extremely proud of their gods and had many myths to tell of their exploits. One of these stories, called the *Enuma Elish*, has within it an account of how Marduk (the chief god of the Babylonians) had conquered and killed the goddess Tiamat and from her body formed the heavens and the earth. In response to this emphasis by the Babylonians, the Priestly school composed its own creation account.

Contrary to the Babylonian accounts which had many gods and goddesses, the Hebrew account depicts only one God "brooding" over the face of unformed chaos. This God is so powerful that creation occurs by a spoken word. It is interesting also that this account is structured around the Sabbath motif which had become so important to the religion and life of the Hebrew people (and, of course, dear to the hearts of the priests). The origin of the Sabbath concept in Israel is not known precisely though several theories have been espoused. The point here is that this concept was used by the Priestly writers to depict creation itself in concert with the Sabbath ideal. God created for six days; on the seventh God rested. Thus the seventh day is as special for God as it is for God's people.

It should be obvious to even a casual reader that this account is very different from that found in 2:4—3:24. Here one finds an orderly creation brought into existence simply by God's "word." There is purpose in the order, and human beings (both male and female here) are given dominion over God's creation. It is said that humans are created in "God's image." Much ink has been spilled over the years in an attempt to understand exactly what that meant. One explanation that merits attention understands an "image" in ancient times to be a representative of a person or figure in a place of high authority. The "image" is entrusted to perform an important task on behalf of the one who commissioned the image. Here human beings are described as created in God's image and given the task of ruling over God's creation. No small task! All of God's work was seen to be "good," i.e., it did what it was created to do.

Some people are confused about why there should be two creation accounts. If one understands the ancient mind-set, however, such confusion can be avoided. Each of these accounts came from different times and strands of tradition, and each functioned differently in those settings. They were then placed at the beginning of the Priestly history to function as religious expressions concerning the creation of the world by God and the subsequent fall of the human race and to set the stage for the consequences of that fall.

Recently there has been a great debate between scientists and "creationists" who want to interpret the biblical accounts as a type of pseudoscience. As sincere as these persons are, such an approach completely misses the point of the biblical stories. These stories do not pretend to tell "how" the world was created in modern scientific terminology; they tell "who" created it and "why." These are the religious questions, and on that basis one can indeed argue for the truth of the biblical writings if one has a faith commitment to the biblical teachings. That faith commitment, however, should not "o'erleap itself" to force on these stories a historical literalism which obviously they do not have. Some sincere people may believe that such ideas are heresy. It is a far greater "heresy," however, to argue that these two accounts say identically the same thing literally, imposing on the biblical editors a stupidity and an almost total lack of understanding with regard to these two stories. Leave the "how" of creation to the scientists (who while they have some interesting theories find that the more they learn about the universe the more their theories have to be revised). The religious understandings are then left to the inspired writers of J and P and the final editors of the Torah. "Myths," or better "myth-type stories," are found among the biblical materials, like it or not!

Another quite popular story type in ancient Israelite tradition was the "theophany." The term literally means an "appearance of God." In these stories the presence of God is depicted in a certain time at a certain place for a particular reason. At exceedingly significant moments in the history of Israel God was present, and this presence was often represented by the element of fire. One recalls the story of God's covenant with Abraham (cf. Gen. 15, especially 15:17), the pillar of fire in the wilderness (cf. Exod. 13:22), the scene at Mt. Sinai (cf. Exod. 19:18), and especially the burning bush where Moses received the call to lead the people out of Egypt (cf. Exod. 3). One finds such stories not only in the Torah but also in other biblical writings.

Law

Most of the materials found in the Torah, however, are concerned with laws and ritual/cultic regulations. The community of Israel obviously believed that it was to be governed by rules and principles which would distinguish it from other peoples. The most famous of the codes of law found in the Torah is that known as the Ten Commandments or the Decalogue. This code is probably very old and formed the foundation for the people of God created by the Exodus event. There are several versions of this code (cf. Exod. 20 and 34, Deut. 5), and one can ascertain by examination of these accounts that different traditions altered the commandments to fit their own situations and understandings. Originally these commands were probably very short and all negative. A brief examination of the Decalogue is helpful for a proper understanding of the original meaning and intent of these directives.

The setting for these commandments is God's deliverance of the Hebrew people from Egypt. The "law" is therefore rooted in an act of God's mercy and grace. Further, one notes that very few specifics are given, but rather principles are presented which were to be used as guidelines for the life of the new covenant community. The most important element for this new people was to be their relationship with God. They were to have no gods before Yahweh. Mosaic religion (as it is sometimes called) was basically henotheistic, i.e., advocating the worship of one god but without denying the existence of others. Such a denial in Hebrew religious thought did not come until the time of the Exile (550 B.C., cf. Isa. 44:6–8; 45:5).

Another peculiarity of Hebrew religion was its resistance to the making of forms or images of Yahweh. One of the key points to remember about Israelite religion was the clear teaching that Yahweh could not be manipulated by human beings. In those days it was believed that in some way the "image" of the god did more than simply "represent" the presence of the god. Having the image meant that the god was at the disposal of the people and could be manipulated by them. The religion of Israel always denied that Yahweh could be so used, even though in the popular mind on numerous occasions the people sometimes believed that they had Yahweh "in their back pocket"! The proscription of idols and the strict injunction not to use Yahweh's name in any unseemly way both underscored God's refusal to be a servant of humankind.

Naturally there was an emphasis on the keeping of the Sabbath as a day specially devoted to the worship of Yahweh. Interestingly enough the reason given for the celebration of the Sabbath is twofold: in the Exodus account the reason lies in God's creative work in six days and resting on the seventh; in Deuteronomy the reason is given as a remembrance of the time when the people were enslaved in Egypt before God led them out from that place. In either case the community of God's people was instructed to celebrate and honor the Sabbath as a witness to its faith.

The remaining commandments basically center in the community's responsibility to other members. God's people had more responsibility than simply relating to Yahweh. They were to relate positively to each other as well. The first of these injunctions was concerned with the family unit and the obligation of children to care for their parents in old age. It was a given of that society that children were to obey and respect their parents. This command emphasizes the continuing responsibility of children for aging parents. The idea was that if a person honored and cared for older parents then the older person would live longer, and then the children, in turn, would also live longer and in security, being cared for by their children.

The prohibition against killing has been misunderstood and misused by persons today who attempt to "proof-text" certain modern ideas. The commandment does *not* prohibit killing in war or in cases of capital punishment. In those times there was no prohibition against the taking of human life, only the taking of human life without some sort of justification approved by the community in unusual circumstances. Human life was considered precious, but protection of the community from external or internal threat was equally important.

The most famous of the commandments is the seventh, or perhaps one should say the breaking of this commandment is practiced most frequently! Adultery in ancient Israel, however, was different from modern understandings. That society was male dominated and this commandment to a certain degree reflects that situation. Adultery was committed only against a husband, not against a wife. If a husband had sexual relations with an unmarried woman, no adultery was involved! If a wife had sexual relations with a man, both she and the man had committed adultery against the woman's husband. This was a capital offense, the offenders to be stoned to death.

There is perhaps a valid cultural reason for the harshness of this practice. In those days, since there was no real concept of life after death except the dim, shadowy existence in Sheol to which all people went at death, it was considered essential for the deceased to have a connection to the land of the living through a physical descendant. Thus the levirate law emerged. This law stipulated that in the event of the death of a husband who had no physical descendants a "nearest of kin" was to impregnate the widow. That child was then considered as actually the child of the deceased husband, and in some way this would alleviate the dreary existence of the departed in Sheol by retaining his link to the land of the living. (Exactly how this was accomplished is never really spelled out, however.) Because of this type of thinking, then, it was very important to insure that the child born to a wife was truly the child of the husband. Strict adherence to the seventh commandment was considered extremely important in such a setting.

The eighth commandment which prohibits stealing may have originated as a deterrent against the stealing of fellow Israelites to be sold into slavery. In its present form, however, the idea centers in respect for the property of others. It was an accepted tenet of life that some persons had more material possessions than others, but this commandment argues for the protection of personal property (if acquired honorably, assuredly). Such a statute would make for a certain stability in the community. It was also recognized in the larger law codes that those who were blessed, materially speaking, had a moral responsibility to assist those who were poor. For example, the law made it clear that when harvesting grain in the fields, not everything was to be taken. Something had to be left for the poor (cf. Lev. 19:9–10; 23:22–25). There were specific directions for care of widows and orphans and the aged. A society that neglects its weaker constituencies cannot be a just or stable society.

A just society also demands a system of laws to insure proper order because it is a fact of human existence that not all people are going to conform to right conduct and not all persons will agree with regard to what is fair and equitable. For this reason the ninth commandment concerns the bearing of false witness in legal proceedings. To bear false witness was to undermine the stabilizing structure of the community, and severe penalties were exacted against those who practiced perjury.

The final commandment is similar in some respects to the eighth, but the human tendency toward covetousness was considered to lie at the heart of many a community's problems. Therefore this "attitude" could manifest itself in many forms some of which are listed in the commandment. Specific examples of this attitude were spelled out in the later laws of the settled community.

The Ten Commandments laid down principles for basic relationships with God and one's neighbor. These rules seem to be very old and lie at the heart of Mosaic religion. A community of persons who claim to be God's special people must be characterized by unique modes of conduct and attitudes, and that group must be a "just" society. Such a society must have guidelines which are straight-forward and consistent and applied equally to all members of the community.

The Holiness Code

Most of the remainder of the materials contained in Exodus, Leviticus, and Numbers consist of "conditional" laws, cultic direc-tives, and modes of behavior which were to characterize God's people. Many persons today wonder about the relevance of many of these laws since they deal with matters no longer appropriate to our soci-ety. Laws regarding diet and proper ritual in sacrifice simply do not concern most contemporary people. The question then becomes one of trying to determine why such directives can still be part of the "authoritative" Word. While the specifics of such directives may well be culturally determined and therefore no longer relevant, there may be, however, some principles and guidelines which are still appro-priate for a community which understands itself as the unique people of God.

Perhaps one of the best guidelines in understanding these mate-rials can be located in the theme of the "Holiness Code" found in Leviticus 17—26. "You shall be holy; for I the LORD your God am holy" (19:2). The word "holy" in Hebrew basically means "other than." Anyone or anything which is "holy" is different, set apart, special. God is "other than" human beings; Yahweh's people are supposed to be different from other peoples. God's people are set apart to be special, and these certain special features cause other people to know that they are different. A second consideration also seems to have been an emphasis upon what is good for the commu-nity and for individuals in the community.

For example, the eating of swine was forbidden. The question as to why this particular meat was not among the accepted entrees is still open. Was it because the Canaanites ate pork? Or were pigs used in the worship of Baal? Or was it because many people who ate uncooked pork became seriously ill? The specific reasons for the prohibition may be forever lost, but the principles are clear. God's people must be different; they must not be associated with pagan practices; they must not do things which are harmful to themselves. While specifics may vary from culture to culture, the principles can still be applied in any society.

The book of Deuteronomy, which was originally the introduction to the Deuteronomic history, comes from a different setting with different traditions from those found in Genesis through Numbers. The book is presented as a farewell sermon (or sermons) delivered by Moses to the people which recapitulates the wilderness wanderings but basically focuses on the covenant made by Yahweh with Israel. In Deuteronomy one finds a second account of the Ten Commandments (5:6–21) and directives which arose out of the covenant made between Yahweh and Israel. There are numerous laws in Deuteronomy not found among the Priestly directives. Deuteronomy and thus the Torah concludes with Moses' death and the Hebrew people poised on the other side of the Jordan awaiting direction from Joshua to enter the promised land. To the Jewish people in Exile in Babylon, when the Deuteronomic history was probably written, this would have awakened in their hearts the hope that perhaps they could some day return home to the land of Judah.

The Torah became an authoritative guideline for the Jewish community somewhere around 400 B.C. At that point in the development of the Jewish faith these people had become a "religion of the book," as it is sometimes called. Up until this time the religious traditions had been passed along originally in oral form but later also in some written sources. These traditions had been used and reused as the needs of the community had changed. Finally at this point the stories and traditions were woven together for the purpose of directing the people in the post-exilic community as to how to be the unique people of God; and further, this account gave them a unified history, i.e., roots, which could be traced back to God's purpose in creation. They were able to see what happens when God's people are obedient, disobedient, and repentant. These were items which spoke directly to the needs of the post-exilic Jewish community. From that day to this the Torah has been *the* basic authoritative document for the Jewish faith.

Suggestions for Further Study

Bailey, Lloyd R. *The Pentateuch*. Nashville: Abingdon Press, 1981. Interpreting Biblical Texts Series. Excellent for methodology.
Brueggemann, Walter. *Genesis: A Bible Commentary for Teaching and Preaching*. Atlanta: John Knox Press, 1982.
Clements, Ronald E. *Exodus*. Cambridge: Cambridge University Press, 1972.
Davidson, Robert. *Genesis 1—11*. Cambridge: Cambridge University Press, 1973.
———. *Genesis 12—50*. Cambridge: Cambridge University Press, 1978.
Snaith, N. H. *Leviticus and Numbers*. London: Thomas Nelson & Sons, 1967.
Phillips, Anthony. *Deuteronomy*. Cambridge: Cambridge University Press, 1973.

III

How to Interpret
Historical Books

Several books in the Bible fall under the heading of "historical writings." This is not to say that there are no historical data in other books such as the Torah, but the primary emphasis of several books is on "history." The modern interpreter must avoid the temptation to equate a present understanding of historiography as basically the presentation of objective facts "as they happened" with ancient understandings of the historical process. The ancients quite frequently believed that history was under the control of the gods and that understanding history was a part of understanding the gods and their purposes in and for the world. History for them, therefore, could not possibly be understood properly apart from a religious orientation.

The Hebrew people were especially sensitive to this understanding of history. One of their fundamental beliefs was that Yahweh was the God of history and was working out divine plans and purposes in and through the historical process. They interpreted history, therefore, in the light of their understanding of Yahweh's will and purposes for them and for the world. Christian writers later understood history in very much the same manner.

Deuteronomic History

One of the major historical works included among the biblical writings has already been mentioned, namely the Deuteronomic history which originally included the books of Deuteronomy, Judges, Samuel, and Kings. While the Priestly history (Gen., Exod., Lev., Num., and Josh.) could also be designated as history, it is perhaps best to understand that work somewhat differently since so much of the material included in the "historical" part (i.e., Gen.) can be classified under different literary categories (myths, sagas, and etiological stories). Laws and regulations then take up most of the remainder of the writing. It is best, then, to understand the Priestly history as a foundational document for the religious community which presents God's purpose for that community and sets out rules and guidelines for the people who have entered into a new relationship with God. The story ranges all the way from creation in Genesis to the settlement of the land in what is now the book of Joshua.

The Deuteronomic history is obviously more an attempt at relating real history than of telling a story with some history included. It begins with the Hebrew people in Egyptian slavery, shows how they were delivered from that sorry state, relates the process of becoming a nation and then of splitting into two nations, gives an account of each nation until its fall, and concludes with the Judean people in Babylonian captivity. It is clear from a study of these books (Deut., Judg., Sam., and Kings) that the author(s) had access to numerous sources in the compilation and composition of this work. These sources probably came from different places and different times and reflected the diverse viewpoints which existed in the course of Israel's history.

For example, there seems to have been in ancient Israel soon after the people entered into the land a loosely knit organization of tribes held together by common allegiance to the God, Yahweh. Such a society is usually designated as an amphictyony. Because these tribes were only recently settled in the land of Canaan, were not centrally organized and administered, and were culturally and economically poor, they were easy prey for other stronger and more well-established groups around them. This situation gave rise to heated discussion concerning whether they ought to be organized together into a larger state with a king to rule over them. This could give them more military and economic power. Naturally there were two schools of thought. One group felt that to have a human king was an act of unbelief, a questioning of the power of Yahweh, which bordered on apostasy. The other group felt that the realities of the world called for strong human leadership which was absolutely essential for the survival of the group and that God could still be worshiped and obeyed even if there were a human king. Both of these ideas are preserved in what was probably two different sources or traditions included in the final redaction of the Deuteronomic books. For example, one can compare the promonarchical account of making Saul king in 1 Samuel 9:1—10:16 with the antimonarchical account in 1 Samuel 8; 10:17–27. Obviously no real problem was felt on the part of the Deuteronomic historians in including both of these sources and viewpoints. It could be that they considered both of these views to have contained some valid points and to illustrate what can happen when either extreme is practiced. After all, the excesses of the monarchy are carefully cited in the remainder of this historical work.

One finds in the Deuteronomic history not only sources or traditions such as those already mentioned with regard to the kingship but specific sources cited such as the book of Jasher (cf. Josh. 10:13 and 2 Sam. 1:18), the book of the Acts of Solomon (cf. 1 Kings 11:41), the book of the Chronicles of the Kings of Israel (cf. 1 Kings 14:19), and the book of the Chronicles of the Kings of Judah (cf. 1 Kings 14:29). The careful reader will also find lists of cities and territories, lists of judges, stories about judges, saga stories (i.e., Samson), ancient poems, stories about Saul, David, the ark, and an old history dealing with the fight over the succession to David's throne (found in 2 Sam. 9—20, 1 Kings 1—2). In all probability other sources and traditions were also used, but these are the most obvious. The use of these varied traditions explain some of the seeming contradictions and differing accounts of the same historical event.

The Deuteronomic Religious Emphases

The primary key to interpreting this work, however, is an understanding of the religious presuppositions of the editor(s) who set the materials into the form which now exists. The Deuteronomic history has its own overarching religious emphases which it has superimposed on the materials. One of these is a major emphasis on the importance and role of the covenant in the structure and order of the Hebrew community. This emphasis is supplemented by another which is quite frequently known as *the* Deuteronomic theology. Simply put the Deuteronomic editors believed that history worked in accord with Yahweh's will and commandments. If the people obey these laws, all will be well with them. If, however, they disobey, judgment and evil will befall them. Understanding this simple idea can help the interpreter to "spot" key ideas in the writings, understand how the materials were structured, and interpret the use of sources included by the editor(s).

For example, the basic structure of the entire Deuteronomic history revolves around whether the people of Yahweh were obedient to Yahweh's covenant. When they were, all was well. When they disobeyed, judgment befell them. One can distinguish the pattern especially in the book of Judges. The people sin; the people are punished; the people cry out in repentance; God delivers them. The pattern is quite frequently designated as apostasy—judgment—repentance—deliverance (cf. Judg. 3:12–30).

The question always arises among sensitive people of faith as to why the history of the Hebrew people was told in this type of religious and literary setting. One can really only conjecture, but since the last part of the history concludes with the king, Jehoiachin, being released from prison in the Babylonian captivity (561 B.C.) it is plausible to assume that the overall work has to do with the historical context at that particular time. The people had rebelled against Yahweh and broken God's covenant. After frequent warnings which were consistently ignored, the judgment came upon the two nations. Israel fell in 722/1 B.C. never to return. The southern kingdom, Judah, fell to the Babylonians in 597 and 586 B.C., with most of the people being carried away to Babylonia as exiles. But, history shows that even though judgment comes upon disobedient people who break the relationship between themselves and God, Yahweh can forgive and restore that broken relationship. This is the hope that the Deuteronomic history holds out to the people. It also stands as a stern warning that evil can come upon the people at any time when they are disobedient and break God's covenant. The lessons of the past must be learned, or the tragedy can recur.

This history was probably written originally for the people in exile but was used later when they returned to the land of Judah (538 B.C.). It was not at first understood to be authoritative or canonical but was probably revered and consulted in addition to the Torah which was accepted as *canon* perhaps as early as 400 B.C. By about 200 B.C. the Deuteronomic history was considered to be authoritative alongside the Torah and by that time a second collection had been attached to this writing, namely the four scrolls containing the prophetic materials.

Joshua

One other item should be discussed in connection with the Deuteronomic history. That concerns the problem of the book of Joshua and its place in that history. As suggested above (cf. p. 37), the Priestly history probably concluded with the book of Joshua, and the Deuteronomic history began with the book of Deuteronomy. When the Torah was put into roughly its present form, the figure of Moses was considered to be dominant with regard to authority for the Hebrew religious community. Since the book of Deuteronomy dealt with Moses and Moses' commands to the people, it seemed natural to take it away from its place at the head of the Deuteronomic history. Since the book of Joshua which concluded the Priestly history dealt with the time after Moses, it was placed where Deuteronomy had been at the head of the Deuteronomic history. After this switch occurred, several Deuteronomic revisions were made on the book of Joshua to accommodate more fully its religious teaching to its new literary setting. This explains, then, why there are two very different accounts of the settlement of the land of Canaan after the Exodus. Joshua depicts basically a military conquest which went rather smoothly, while Judges depicts a slow settlement in the land which did not always go smoothly. If one realizes that these two books came from different historical overviews with somewhat different religious viewpoints, the presence of these two different accounts is much more understandable.

Reading through the Deuteronomic history, the student can readily understand that, while "facts" are important to these writers, the most important dimension in the recitation of the history is the religious interpretation of these facts. The absolute facticity of these events and the absolute "chronological correctness" of the accounts are not the primary concern of these historians. Religious understandings and interpretations of that history constitute the fundamental concern of these people, for the religious principles derived from and sometimes imposed upon their "history" continued to be relevant for God's people.

The Work of the Chronicler

A second historical survey appeared in the post-exilic period, perhaps about 350–300 B.C. This work is usually designated as having been compiled by someone (or a group) known as the "Chronicler." It consists of 1 and 2 Chronicles and the books of Ezra and Nehemiah. Originally there were only two larger books, but these were later divided into four. This work shows some affinities to the Priestly work which formed the structure for the books of Genesis, Exodus, Leviticus, Numbers, and Joshua. In this account, however, the emphasis lies in the centrality of the temple with its cultic apparatus for the life of the religious community.

If one understands the historical background for the post-exilic Jewish community in Judah, the emphasis of the Chronicler's work becomes much clearer. In 539 B.C. Cyrus the Persian defeated the Babylonian Empire and then allowed the exiled peoples in Babylon to return to their homelands and to worship their own gods. Therefore, in 538 B.C. some of the Jewish people of Babylon returned to Judah. What they found was depressing: a basically uninhabited countryside with any good areas already claimed by others; Jerusalem in ruins and uninhabited; and, of course, the old temple still in ruins. These people had no political power, little economic resources, and no means to protect themselves from outsiders who could (and sometimes did) attack them at will. Discouraging words were frequently heard!

After a while, at the urging of the prophets Haggai and Zechariah, a new temple was built (520–515 B.C.). Since the people were not organized into a political state (they were part of the Persian system of government), the temple, proper worship, and later, adherence to the Torah became the distinguishing marks of this community. Some call this societal structure a "theocracy," a community ruled by religion and the leaders of the religion, in this case the priests.

The Chronicler (whether one person or a number of persons is not known) compiled a history of the Hebrew people from the time of Adam to the time of Ezra and Nehemiah. In reading the material one can determine almost immediately that precise historical detail is not the Chronicler's strong suit either. He proceeds from Adam to David simply by listing a genealogy. Interestingly enough, in this account David is highly idealized not as a political figure but as the one who made great preparation for the building of the temple. This is reflective of the fact that at that moment in Judah's history there were no Davidic heirs to sit upon a political throne, and thus the new community was presented as centering in the temple which was understood to be the great legacy of David. Thus the new community was tied together with the old. The true people of God were still standing in the ancient traditions.

It is clear that the Chronicler understood that the people of God in that moment of history were those who were living in Judah whose lives revolved around the temple. This is seen in the way the author or editor emphasizes the Southern Kingdom. For example, after the division of the Solomonic state into northern Israel and southern Judah in 922/1 B.C., Israel is not mentioned again! It is interesting also to note that very few of the kings of Judah are mentioned, and only those who had some special connection with the temple are discussed (David, Solomon, Jehoshaphat, Hezekiah, and Josiah).

The books of Chronicles, then, appear to be rewrites of the old Priestly history and the Deuteronomic history. The books of Ezra and Nehemiah, however, contain some new material and take the reader into the post-exilic Jewish community in Judah. There is evidence of the use of sources in the Chronicler's composition especially in these latter two books, Ezra-Nehemiah. It appears that there may have been two sources, one dealing with Ezra and one with Nehemiah which were inserted into the account but without regard to chronological sequence. As the account presently stands Ezra and Nehemiah were basically contemporaries, but upon closer examination it becomes very probable with regard to chronology that Nehemiah preceded Ezra in his work with the people in Judah. Again historical accuracy was not a primary concern to those persons as it is to modern writers of history.

The Chronicler's account was written to demonstrate to the Jewish people of the post-exilic community how to retain their traditions and how to act as the unique people of God in their new circumstances. Adherence to the traditions, especially those connected with the temple, was especially important. Also the account was presented to demonstrate that a political state was not necessary for the continued existence of the community. Even though David had been presented as a great political figure in the Deuteronomic history, the Chronicler presented David as great because of his relationship with the temple. And it was around the temple that the life of the post-exilic community revolved.

Again one finds a classic illustration of how the biblical writers used history to learn lessons from the past to speak to the contemporary needs of the faith community. The objective data were not as important as the religious interpretations presented in the materials. Once the interpreter understands that aspect of the historical presentations of the biblical writers, principles and guidelines can be found in the texts which can be appropriated for present situations also. The principle emphases of the Chronicler that the community of God's people is to be different, is to preserve its unique character, and is to be centered in proper worship of God can even now be applied and appreciated. Religious principles can be applied to new and/or modified cultural and historical settings.

Acts

The last of the "histories" contained in the Bible is found in the book of Acts. Actually this book is only the second part of a two-volume work which began with the Gospel of Luke. Since the Gospel genre will be discussed later (cf. pp. 90ff.), the concentration here will be upon the book of Acts which appears to be a history of the early Christian community in Jerusalem and how it spread over the Greco-Roman world.

The author of Luke-Acts obviously had some reason for telling the story as he did, as did the compilers of the Deuteronomic history and the Chronicler. The early Christian church was at first understood to be only a sect movement within Judaism. The growth of the Christian movement, while steady, was slow, and numerically speaking the church was small. The group met together in the homes of members. It was probably an asset for the Christians at that time to be considered as part of the multifaceted Judaism of the Greco-Roman period. War broke out, however, between the Jewish people in Palestine and the Romans (A.D. 66), and when the smoke of battle had cleared, the Romans had sacked Jerusalem and at least partially (if not fully) destroyed the temple. This final defeat came in A.D. 70. By this time the Christian movement had established itself as an entity in itself, and in the light of the recent unpleasantness between Judaism and the Roman Empire the Christians probably wished to dissociate themselves from Judaism. The work, Luke-Acts, was probably written shortly after A.D. 70 at least in part to show to the Roman world that Christians were not trouble makers but were loyal citizens of the Roman state. While Christians talked of a king and of a kingdom, these were of a different order from the political understandings of most people.

The author of Luke-Acts intended to present a "history" depicting the growth of the Christian church, but it was history in the same sense as those presented in the old Deuteronomic history and the work of the Chronicler. Interestingly enough many of the Greeks and Romans wrote history in much the same way but for different purposes, of course, (cf. the works of Herodotus, Thucydides, Suetonius, and Tacitus for some illustrations). In this literary work the author presented several emphases which the interpreter finds throughout both Luke and Acts. The major themes which should be noted in Acts are (1) the universality of the new religion, Christianity, that it is for all people of the world, Jew and Gentile, male and female alike; and (2) the political innocence of the Christian movement and of the leaders of the early Christian church (Jesus included).

What is being written in this presentation is "theological history." It has been structured around Acts 1:8: "but you shall receive power when the Holy Spirit has come upon you; and you shall be my witnesses in Jerusalem and in all Judea and Samaria and to the end of the earth." The first part of the book depicts the beginnings of the church in Jerusalem with opposition from the Jewish authorities. A persecution finally erupts, driving most of the Christians into the larger area of Palestine with Antioch in Syria gradually becoming the center for the church as Acts describes the movement. The majority of the space is devoted, however, to the taking of the Christian message to the Greco-Roman world by the man who became known as the Apostle Paul. He founded churches in Asia Minor, Macedonia, Greece, and finally went to Rome (as a prisoner) where he preached "about the Lord Jesus Christ quite openly and unhindered" (28:31).

The author of Luke-Acts used sources as did the author(s) of the Priestly and Deuteronomic histories and also as did the Chronicler. There is probably no absolute consensus as to the sources which were used but at least three or four seem to be plausible. Sources which may have originated in the early Christian communities in Jerusalem and in Syrian Antioch may have formed the basis for the early chapters of Acts. A source outlining some of Paul's journeys and escapades may possibly also have existed and been utilized. The most interesting possibility for a source used by the author to compose Acts is that of a travel diary kept by a companion of Paul on some of his journeys. In Acts 16—28 one finds several passages where the author shifts from a narrative, "they said, did, etc." to a personal "we said, did, etc." (cf. 16:9–18; 20:5–15[16–38]; 21:1–18; 27:1—28:16). Some scholars have argued that these "we" passages corroborate the historicity of these events, having come from an eyewitness. Other scholars disagree. It is not the purpose here to debate that issue, but one notes with interest that the religious interpretations and emphases of the "we" passages are the same as those in the remainder of Acts.

That the book of Acts was not intended as a comprehensive history can be clearly ascertained by a careful study of the book itself. There is no mention of most of the Apostles, what they did or where they went. The two central figures are Peter and Paul. How the church began and developed in many parts of the Roman Empire was largely ignored. The emphasis here, as with the other biblical histories, is upon religious ideology, not absolute accuracy. There is at some points corroboration of the Acts account when it is compared with certain statements made in Paul's letters. There are, however, some points at which the Acts account and Paul cannot be made to fit together. One confronts such a problem when one compares Paul's account of his visits to Jerusalem (Galatians 1—2) with the accounts of Acts (9—15, especially). All of this is simply to point out the obvious: that historical writings in the Bible are not only composed to relay "facts," but more importantly they were written to present the theological or religious meaning of those events which had been experienced and interpreted by the faith community. The arrangement of the material was done for that purpose, not to present a precise chronology of "what happened." To the biblical writers "what happened" by itself was not important. The religious interpretations and understandings of what happened were.

Suggestions for Further Study

Ackroyd, Peter R. *The First Book of Samuel*. Cambridge: Cambridge University Press, 1971.
———. *The Second Book of Samuel*. Cambridge: Cambridge University Press, 1977.
Coggins, R. J. *The Books of Ezra and Nehemiah*. Cambridge: Cambridge University Press, 1976.
———. *The First and Second Books of the Chronicles*. Cambridge: Cambridge University Press, 1976.
Fretheim, Terence E. *Deuteronomic History*. Nashville: Abingdon Press, 1983. Interpreting Biblical Texts Series.
Gray, John. *Joshua, Judges, and Ruth*. London: Thomas Nelson & Sons, 1967.
Packer, J. W. *Acts of the Apostles*. Cambridge: Cambridge University Press, 1966.
Robinson, J. *The First Book of Kings*. Cambridge: Cambridge University Press, 1972.
———. *The Second Book of Kings*. Cambridge: Cambridge University Press, 1976.
Williams, C. S. C. *A Commentary on the Acts of the Apostles*. Second ed. London: Adam and Charles Black, 1964.

IV

How to Interpret
the Prophets

To interpret properly the books containing the prophetic materials, the student must first understand something about the prophets—who they were, what they did, how they understood themselves, and how they were understood in their own times. The prophetic materials comprise the second part of the second division of the Hebrew canon. These are the scrolls of Isaiah, Jeremiah, Ezekiel, and the book of the Twelve (usually designated "minor" prophets because of the shortness of the books).

In older times these prophets were labeled "writing prophets" because these books contain written accounts of the teachings of the various prophetic personalities. Upon closer examination, however, it became clear that these men did not write down their teachings in a book, but rather they were proclaimers of God's message to the community of faith in that time and place. The people usually did not heed their messages, but some persons obviously felt that the teachings of these inspired men were valuable enough to preserve. Thus the sayings or oracles of these proclaimers were preserved in oral form for many years, in some cases many centuries. One of the reasons why the sayings could be preserved was that the prophets delivered their messages in poetic form. They used certain literary forms as well, some of which are identified by scholars as the messenger formula, the threat, the reproach, exhortations, laments, lawsuits, hymns, and dialogues. This allowed those who preserved the traditions to remember them more easily and to pass them along to later generations.

Somewhere along the way the oral traditions were gathered into groups of sayings held together by theme or "catchword" (i.e., a series of sayings in which a certain word like "justice" or "covenant loyalty" was central to the oracles). These collections later came to be written down, and out of such materials the books as they now exist were edited and designed by persons who felt that these teachings should not be lost. This process probably took place in the post-exilic period, culminating by about 200 B.C.

Most modern persons have come to understand "a prophet" as someone who basically is able to predict the future. This understanding has been all too often uncritically applied to the prophetic figures of the Bible. If one reads the prophetic books, however, set against the backdrop of the prophets' times and places, it becomes apparent that they understood themselves to be called to deliver God's message to the people *then and there*. Occasionally the prophets did venture out into predicting the future, but the future they predicted was always the "immediate" future, what was going to happen to the nation and to the people if they did or did not heed God's message. To understand the prophetic books and messages, therefore, one must be acquainted with the history and setting for the prophetic activity. Also each prophet must be studied against his own time and place.

Religiously speaking, the prophets were much akin to the Deuteronomic historians in their basic thinking. They saw that the nations had sinned against God, and thus they told the people that God's judgment was coming upon them. At some points the prophets held out the hope that if the people would repent, they could be delivered from that judgment. But repentance ultimately lost out to disobedience. The basic religious teaching of the prophetic messages is quite similar to the Deuteronomic ideology in its emphasis upon the centrality of the covenant and the nation's responsibility to keep its obligations to that covenant—or else!

Stages of Development

Several stages appear in the development of the prophetic movement. Naturally there was a long period of preparation in older times in which numerous streams began to flow together to form the main river of prophecy in Israel. The prophetic period as commonly understood probably began with the figure of Elijah (869–850 B.C.) during the reign of Ahab in the Northern Kingdom of Israel. Here one finds the solitary figure who felt called by God to deliver God's message to the nation. Some of their messages struck fear into the hearts of the people. The reason for this lay in the belief of those times that there was power resident in the spoken word. Whenever something was said (or done) in a solemn manner, the word unleashed power which would bring the intent of the saying (or action) to fruition. Thus when the prophet proclaimed doom on the nation in the name of Yahweh, that saying had potential for great destruction.

The prophets also performed certain actions which are known as "prophetic signs." Something would be done on a small scale which would bring the larger intent to completion, Jeremiah's breaking of the flask, for example (cf. Jer. 19). The prophets did not, however, do such signs (or deliver messages of doom) at their own whim. They believed that they were doing the will of Yahweh and were acting on Yahweh's command.

After the early stage of the prophetic movement culminating in the careers of Elijah and Elisha, the "classical" prophetic era emerged. This era is usually divided into three periods: the pre-exilic period (850–586 B.C.); the exilic period (586–539 B.C.); and the post-exilic period (538–300 B.C.). Each of these stages had its peculiar emphases which emerged from the historical settings of the times.

In the pre-exilic period the basic message of the prophets was that of *doom*—the nation had broken God's covenant and laws; the nation would be punished. When the first of the prophets, Amos and Hosea, emerged to preach to the Northern Kingdom, Israel, that nation had already gone beyond the point of no return. Their message was simple: Israel will be destroyed; its people carried into Exile in foreign lands; and that nation will not return. In the Southern Kingdom, Judah, the message was similar but somewhat different since the first prophets of the south (Isaiah and Micah) felt that it was not yet too late to repent. If repentance came, the people of Judah could even yet escape the fate of Israel.

Toward the end of the seventh century, however, the situation in Judah had degenerated to the point where the prophets then predicted destruction for the land and for Jerusalem (cf. Jer., Hab., and Zeph.). The leaders and the people failed to heed these spokesmen for God, and that caused the punishment to be much more severe than it would have been (cf. especially Jer.). The land was devastated; the city of Jerusalem destroyed, along with the temple. This occurred in two stages, the first in 597 B.C. and the second in 586 B.C. The people, most of them, were carried off into Babylonia and settled there. Judah ceased to exist as a nation.

During the Exile three prophets spoke to the people in Babylon. Jeremiah, who had remained in Judah, wrote letters to the people there; Ezekiel, who had been carried off after the first conquest by Babylonia in 597 B.C., worked among the people in Exile; and the prophet whose sayings are preserved for us in Isaiah 40–55 who told the people that they were about to be allowed to return home. Jeremiah and Ezekiel coming near the beginning of the Exile advised the people to settle down and make new lives for themselves within their new cultural setting. The last, sometimes called Deutero-Isaiah, ridiculed the Babylonian gods and correctly perceived that Cyrus the Persian was about to destroy the Babylonian Empire. The prophet believed that Cyrus would then allow the Jewish people to return to Judah and begin again to accomplish the tasks which God had called them to fulfill, that of being a "light to the nations."

After the return (though not all the people wanted to return and many, in fact, remained in Babylon) the people expected marvelous things to happen for them quickly and with little effort. Such did not transpire causing the people to be discouraged and disillusioned. The prophets of the post-exilic period tried to encourage the people to be loyal to Yahweh, to keep faith and not to lose heart, and to warn them that disobedience could and would bring punishment again. The message of the post-exilic prophetic personalities (Hag., Zech., Mal., Joel, Isa. 56—66), while still appropriate for certain aspects of the life of the post-exilic community, began to lose its broader appeal and its "steam." The historical situation in which the prophetic movement had flourished was no longer extant and the influence of the prophets began to wane.

The reason for what many scholars call the "decline" of the prophetic movement in the post-exilic community lies in the simple fact that the message of the prophets did not really "fit" into the historical realities of those times. Since the prophetic ideology was basically Deuteronomic, that pattern of thought did not correspond with the realities of the period. This community had been punished for its sins, but now that it had been restored in the land and the people were trying diligently to obey Yahweh's commands, their situation was not improving. In fact on many occasions it had become worse. The old religious teaching was no longer relevant. It did not correspond with reality.

Because of this situation, there developed in the post-exilic community two major movements which could wrestle with these problems. They were the wisdom and the apocalyptic movements. These two movements produced some interesting literature, and some of that literature was incorporated into the Old Testament canon. (These will be described and discussed in the following two chapters.) With the rise of these newer ideologies and the historical realities of that moment, the prophetic movement gracefully faded away, having contributed its part to the richness of the religious traditions of the Hebrew people.

Writing Down the Prophetic Teachings

The individual emphases of the various prophets are far too many to enumerate here, and other books deal with these specifics (cf. bibliography at the conclusion of this chapter). Nevertheless, several points remain to be made to enable the interpreter to understand the prophetic writings better. The first concerns an understanding of the way the prophetic books were put into the form in which most are familiar to people today. Some discussion has already been made about this point (cf. above, p. 48), but additional points need to be clarified. As already noted, the prophets were primarily speakers, and their sayings were preserved and passed along orally for many years. In this process some of the oracles were joined together into shorter groups of sayings dealing with the similar themes, historical circumstances, biographical data, etc. These groups were then used in the final editing process to present the teachings of the prophets in a form which would not only preserve their teachings but which would also speak to the needs of the community in post-exilic Judah.

Because the people then needed to hear some words of hope and encouragement, most of these prophetic books were edited to present a collection of oracles proclaiming doom and judgment against the nation (i.e., Israel or Judah), then a collection of oracles against foreign nations (not in all prophetic books, however), and finally a concluding section which spoke of restoration and renewal of the covenant between God and the people. If there were prophets who did not have words of hope originally, later oracles of hope were added to their teachings. This appears to have been what has happened, for example, with the book of Amos.

The prophet Amos was a Judean who preached to the Northern Kingdom of Israel about 750 B.C. He believed that the nation had become so corrupt that it would be destroyed with little to show that there was once a nation there (cf. Amos 3:12). That teaching is very consistent throughout the collection of oracles, but when one comes to 9:8c–15 the tone changes. Here one finds, especially in 9:11–15, a passage which talks of restoration. This restoration, however, if one looks carefully at the text, is directed toward Judah and the restoration of the Davidic kingship. It would certainly have been out of place for Amos to deliver such an oracle to Israel. The consensus among scholars, therefore, is that these last verses are an oracle of hope delivered in the exilic or post-exilic period to Judah. The question then becomes for the interpreter: why was it placed at the end of Amos' teachings?

The answer to that question lies in the time when these books were finally edited. Here the community was struggling to survive, looking to the teachings of the past for instruction and guidance. That instruction and guidance came very clearly from Amos' teachings: God's people must keep their covenant with God, or they risk the loss of being God's people. The more pressing question for the historical moment, however, was whether there could really be forgiveness after judgment. The last verses of the book of Amos as finally edited urged definitely that there could be, assuming that the people remained repentant and carried out their duties to God and to each other properly. The fact that the last verses refer to Judah was not really relevant, for the major question was that of preserving

God's people whoever and wherever they might be. And these books were edited for the people in Judah.

Contemporary society does not think so much in collective terms as did ancient society. The individual and the individual's fate and preservation are primary considerations for modern persons. Ancient people, however, emphasized the continuation of the group with its unique traditions and customs. That group known as God's people, located now in Judah was destined to continue, as the final editors of Amos (and the other prophetic books) demonstrated by their redaction of the book. The question often asked by modern interpreters concerns who was right about Israel: Amos or the final editors who added the last verses. The answer is that both were right: Amos in correctly seeing that the nation of Israel would never be restored, the redactors in believing that the people of God would somehow survive and continue the traditions and customs of the Hebrew heritage. Though this may seem a bit unusual for modern thinking, it is the responsibility of the modern interpreter to understand the ancient documents as the ancients did. If one can learn to think collectively, the task will be easier to accomplish.

Several other areas should be considered with regard to understanding properly the prophetic teachings. One of these is closely related to the issue just discussed, the restoration of the people in the land of Judah, and it is also connected with the ideas of those who interpret these ancient spokesmen for God as predictors of the future. For example, some theories have been espoused rather strongly in this century which view the prophetic materials as describing modern history, nations, and events. The term which has sometimes been used in connection with this type of thinking is "prewritten history," i.e., the prophets wrote *our* modern history in *their* time. The idea is that significant events of the modern world and in contemporary history have all been recorded beforehand in the prophetic messages. All current events are then examined and prophetic passages championed as having already predicted these occurrences. One such event, and a crucial one, is the establishment of the modern state of Israel. Now the merits or demerits of the creation of the state of Israel in 1948 are not at issue here. Others more knowledgeable will have to argue those positions. The central point to be made here is that the old prophets had *absolutely nothing* to say about that situation.

Numerous references in the prophetic books speak to the point of God's people being settled in the land of Judah again and becoming a political state. If one reads the biblical accounts with an understanding of those times and of the fact that the prophets spoke to the people then and there, it becomes evident that what they meant was the return of the people from Babylonia, the re-establishment of the people in the land and Jerusalem, and the creation of the people into a renewed political entity. The people returned from Babylonia 538 B.C.; they settled in Judah and began to try to establish a new community which they ultimately did with the help of Nehemiah and Ezra between 444 and about 400 B.C.; and they became a significant political entity again after the Maccabean era 141–63(40) B.C. All those "predictions" (which were contingent in the first place) have already come to pass. Nothing in any of those texts in any way remotely refers to the modern state of Israel. Use of the biblical materials in this way as justification for modern political movements is really an illegitimate use of those texts.

Did the Prophets Predict Jesus?

Another popular misinterpretation of the prophetic messages concerns Christian ideas with regard to how the prophets "predicted" Jesus. Many have the notion that the prophetic books are filled with predictions of the Messiah and that Jesus fulfilled these predictions specifically in every detail. The truth is that this long-held and popular understanding is false. In the first place there are really very few references in the prophets to a "Messiah." And further, these references do not envision a person who would come in the distant future but in the prophet's immediate future. Finally, an additional problem concerns the figure of the "servant of Yahweh" in Isaiah 40—55: was this person intended or understood to be messianic? These three areas will be examined briefly here to demonstrate how these materials should be interpreted.

One finds, upon examination of the prophetic writings, that the prophets quite frequently placed their hope for a repentant community or nation in the figure of the king. The king was supposed to represent the people and to lead them in proper worship and action. Whenever there was a bad king, the prophet would begin to look forward to a new king who would be like David to lead the people and to establish the kingdom in a secure and responsible manner. David was looked upon as a great leader (which he was), but an idealization process had taken place so that the Davidic kingship was looked upon as an idyllic period when all was positive in the land.

In Israel three groups of persons were called to duties and tasks and set apart for those tasks by being anointed with oil. These three were the priests, the prophets, and the kings. In the period of the kingdoms in Israel's history, it was naturally a very significant event when the king was anointed since so much of the peace, prosperity, and well-being of the people was focused in that person. The word in the Hebrew for "anoint" is *msh*, and the noun form from that word is *messi^{a}h*, the anointed one. Thus the term *Messiah* refers to an anointed one, usually the king. It is not surprising then to learn that in days when there was a bad king, the heart of the prophet and people looked forward to a new, good king who would lead the people rightly as David (the idealized David) had done. The new king was a *Messiah*. Thus that idea and concept was basically political when it first began.

Scholars have argued for many years about the timing of the messianic concept, that is, specifically, did it arise in the pre-exilic period when there were bad kings or in the post-exilic period when there was no king? The definitive answer to that question has not been found, but in either case the idea shows a longing for a good king to lead the people of God. The assumption which will be used here is the former, that the idea of Messiah began in the pre-exilic period and re-emerged during periods when there were bad kings.

Several examples demonstrate certain understandings of the concept in the prophets' own times. Isaiah 9:2–7 is *a* or perhaps *the* classic passage describing the Messiah. The historical setting for this passage lies in eighth-century Judah during the reign of Ahaz. This king was weak, religiously speaking, and Isaiah looked forward to a new king who would be what a king was supposed to be. This passage then may have been delivered when Hezekiah, Ahaz's son, was born or (more probably) when he ascended to the throne in 715 B.C. The description given is that of a good king, and the attributes assigned to him reflect the ideas of kingship at that time: Wonderful Counselor, Mighty Warrior, Everlasting Father (or better, Father for a long time), Prince of Peace (well-being). Of the increase of his government and of peace there would be no end. This is obviously a religio-political description of the king in those times, not the prediction of someone to come hundreds of years later. A similar description in chapter 11 parallels the teaching in 9:2–7. Another passage from a prophet contemporary with Isaiah, namely Micah, also reflects the same kind of teaching (cf. Mic. 5:2–4).

This teaching emphasizing a Messiah is not found, however, in the majority of the prophetic books. Jeremiah refers to a "Branch" which appears to be similar to Isaiah's teaching (cf. Jer. 23:5), and Ezekiel speaks about a new shepherd to lead Yahweh's sheep (Ezek. 34:23–24). After the Exile Zechariah spoke about a Branch (Zech. 3:8), but he appears to have someone specific in mind, a certain Zerubbabel, who very soon disappeared from the scene. Other than those, there are very few references (cf. perhaps also Zech. 9:9; 12:10) to anyone who could be looked upon as a "Messiah," and there are certainly no references to a figure of the distant future. These passages must be understood against the background of their own times, and the primary meaning must be understood in those contexts.

One other passage is frequently cited and also debated in regard to messianism. That passage is Isaiah 7:14, which is found in the larger context of Isaiah 7:1—8:15. The setting of this passage, historically speaking, comes from 734 B.C. when the king of Assyria, Tiglath-pileser III, was threatening the northern nations of Palestine including Syria and Israel. These two nations had banded together and were attempting to enlist all the smaller nations in the area to join them in an effort to keep Assyria away. Judah was being pressured to join this alliance, known as the Syro-Ephraimitic alliance. Ahaz did not want to join and fight against the Assyrians; therefore, he was seriously contemplating appealing to Assyria for aid, to become a political vassal of that state.

Such an action was repugnant to the prophets because in those days not only did a vassal state have to pay tribute to the superior, furnish men for service in those armies, and sometimes furnish women for concubines, but they also had to worship, at least nominally, the gods of the superior nation. When Ahaz was debating whether to appeal to Tiglath-pileser III, Isaiah went to the king in an attempt to dissuade him from that course of action. One of the stories in this section deals with a sign which was to be given to Ahaz to encourage him to remain loyal to Yahweh, not to appeal to Assyria for aid. The literal translation of the Hebrew text of Isaiah 7:14–16 is this: "Behold the young woman is already pregnant and is about to bear a child, and shall call his name Immanuel [meaning, God is with us]. . . . For before the child knows how to refuse the evil and choose the good, the land before whose two kings you are in dread will be deserted."

Thus, this is not a prediction of someone to come in the distant future but a child about to be born. Knowing the difference between right and wrong for a child in those days was usually understood to be somewhere between two and twelve years of age. In other words, Isaiah was saying that in a very short while the nations of Syria and Israel would be gone. The date of this incident in Isaiah's life is usually understood to be 734 B.C. Syria fell to the Assyrians in 732 B.C. and Israel in 722/1 B.C. Isaiah was, to use an old expression, right on the money. This passage is set within a context of deliverance, God's deliverance of the people from a grave danger. Interestingly enough, Ahaz appealed to Assyria in spite of Isaiah's pleas not to do so, and in future years this cost the people of Judah dearly.

Some may rightly ask just why this passage (and others) has been used by the New Testament writers and seen by them to have been "fulfilled" in Jesus. A discussion of this topic would take us far afield from the principle task at hand, but suffice it to say here that "fulfillment" in the minds of the New Testament writers was not the same as a literal prediction coming true. For the most part the New Testament writers found "fulfillment" on a different level than the literal. For example, the passage just examined in Isaiah 7:14 is cited in Matthew 1:23 with reference to the birth of Jesus. If one reads Matthew carefully, it becomes very clear that for him the most important dimension in the coming of Jesus was God's act of deliverance. Joseph was told, "You shall call his name Jesus, for he will save his people from their sins" (Matt. 1:21). There is certainly a fulfillment seen here by the New Testament writer, but it is a fulfillment which takes place at an "essential" level, not at a literal or superficial level. Such an interpretation as that made by the Gospel writer then obviates the necessity of trying to force a prediction and meaning on Isaiah 7:14 which is obviously not there originally. Care must be taken always to understand how the New Testament writers used the Scriptures and not force modern ideas upon them which were not intended.

The Servant of Yahweh

In this same general category is the teaching found in Isaiah 40—55 which centers in the figure usually designated as the Servant of Yahweh. This figure is found throughout these chapters of the book of Isaiah, and perhaps more ink has been spilled in the discussion of this question than of any other one problem in Old Testament studies. For example, some scholars believe that there are four "servant songs" incorporated in Isaiah 40—55 which should be understood and interpreted separately from other references to the Servant. These passages are usually designated as 42:1-4; 49:1-6; 50:4-11; 52:13—53:12. Unanimity of opinion, however, is hard to find about any aspect of the Servant problem, and scholars do not always agree even on the verses for these four passages. Other problems abound also such as who is the Servant? is the Servant a person or a group or both? did the same author who wrote the songs deliver the other oracles in this section?

These questions cannot be solved simply, but the interpreter must be aware of these problems and attempt to understand these passages in their historical context. If one reads Isaiah 40—55, it seems clear that the Servant is a designation for Israel, the people of God. It is also clear that the suffering of the nation in Exile (these chapters come from the period of the Babylonian captivity, between 550 and 540 B.C.) is understood in some way as vicarious, i.e., undeserved suffering which can have redemptive possibilities for others. Exactly how this was to be understood is not made explicit in the text, however. The concept is firmly set, nevertheless, in the religious understanding of the prophet.

The New Testament writers interpreted Jesus against the background of this Servant figure. This is certainly understandable, given the events of Jesus' ministry, and it is no surprise to learn that their understanding was that Jesus "fulfilled" this concept and these passages. That is different, however, from arguing that the prophet of Isaiah 40—55 predicted Jesus' ministry and Passion. What happened here was that the idea or principle of vicarious suffering came to a climax in the Christian interpretation of Jesus and what happened to him. It was only natural that the early Christians described what had happened to Jesus with regard to analogous types of teaching found in their Scriptures, the teachings of Isaiah 40—55 being essentially the only place in the law and prophets to present such a theology.

What one finds in the prophetic teachings are specific messages proclaimed primarily to the nations of Israel and Judah. These messages were revered, remembered, and passed along by persons who did not wish them to be lost, for they believed that the quality of these teachings was of lasting value which deserved to be preserved for future generations. In the course of time these sayings were finally placed together in "book" form for two reasons: (1) to preserve the teachings of the inspired servants of God; and (2) to use these teachings to challenge and instruct the community in existence at that moment of history. The later community came to accept these documents as authoritative for the faith and practice of all generations.

In reading these prophetic documents the interpreter must keep in mind the historical background of the prophet in his own time and place and also the meaning and use of the prophetic utterances as they were written down in new situations for later generations. If this can be done, the greatness of the prophetic personalities can be appreciated, their messages understood (for each one had individual emphases which went beyond the simple Deuteronomic theology), and faulty interpretations of these writings which are so widespread in contemporary society can be avoided.

Suggestions for Further Study

Efird, James M. *Jeremiah—Prophet Under Siege.* Valley Forge, Pa.: Judson Press, 1979.
————. *The Old Testament Prophets Then and Now.* Valley Forge, Pa.: Judson Press, 1982.
Holladay, William L. *Isaiah: Scroll of Prophetic Heritage.* Grand Rapids, Mich.: Wm. B. Eerdmans Publishing Co., 1978.
Mason, Rex. *The Books of Haggai, Zechariah, and Malachi.* Cambridge: Cambridge University Press, 1977.
Mays, James L. *Ezekiel, Second Isaiah.* Philadelphia: Fortress Press, 1978.
McKeating, Henry. *The Books of Amos, Hosea, and Micah.* Cambridge: Cambridge University Press, 1971.
Ward, James M. *The Prophets.* Nashville: Abingdon Press, 1982. Interpreting Biblical Texts Series.
Watts, John D. W. *The Books of Joel, Obadiah, Jonah, Nahum, Habakkuk, and Zephaniah.* Cambridge: Cambridge University Press, 1975.

V

How to Interpret Wisdom

One of the most delightful components, literarily speaking, of
the biblical materials is wisdom literature and teachings. Every society, aware of it or not, has a wisdom movement within it, for wisdom is basically the quest to understand the world and, thereby, to
learn how to cope with the world and its ways. Most wisdom movements begin as very practical, observing the world and learning how
to stay out of danger and how to use the regulations of the world for
one's personal (or corporate) benefit. In its earliest state, wisdom
takes the form of practical teachings given by a parent to a child or
teachers to students. The primary idea in wisdom teaching is that if
one lives in accordance with the principles of the world and uses
these principles wisely and properly, that person's life will be successful, happy, and filled with good things. Conversely, if a person
defies the principles of the world and tries to make the world conform to individual whim or preference, that person's life will be
filled with problems and unhappiness.

Wisdom movements flourished in the ancient world, especially
in Egypt and Mesopotamia. Interestingly enough this movement was
late in blossoming in Israel. It was probably not until the time of the
United Kingdom under David and Solomon that the "wise man" became an official part of the Hebrew societal structure. Solomon especially supported the wise men in his court, and because of this, all

wisdom in Israel was understood in some way to go back to Solomon (as the law to Moses and prophecy to Elijah). The category of wisdom was much broader perhaps in ancient culture than in modern society. The concept of wisdom in those days could connote someone who was intellectually brilliant or who had studied long and accumulated many details about one or more topics, much as present understandings. But wisdom for that society could also indicate persons who had special skills such as the ability to sense peculiar turns in the course of human life or talents which could enable a person to perform tasks in a successful manner.

The reason for the slow development of the wisdom movement in Israel is perhaps best explained when one recalls that the basic theology of earlier times was Deuteronomic. This religious ideology was remarkably similar in principle to the basic concept in practical wisdom. If one were obedient to God, a good life would be the reward; if one were disobedient to God, evil would surely come. Practical wisdom basically taught that if one acted in accordance with the "laws" of the world, a good life would ensue; if one ignored these principles of life, misfortune would surely come. Since the Hebrews believed that one could not separate the secular from the religious in life, the ideas were practically identical. Since the Deuteronomic theology was so prevalent in early Israel, wisdom while certainly present, did not flourish.

Interestingly enough most wisdom movements had two branches, the practical branch, naturally, but another also. The second branch emerged because it is clear from the observation of life that the first is not always true. Good people who play "by the rules" do not always have good lives, and evil people who ignore or even arrogantly flaunt the rules sometimes have very successful lives. Therefore, a more philosophical or speculative dimension to the wisdom movement arose which attempted to wrestle with the questions of fairness and justice in the world and with the question of whether life makes any sense or has any real meaning.

Because of the similarity between practical wisdom and Deuteronomic theology, then, the wisdom movement in Israel did not really flower until the post-exilic era (after 538 B.C.) when the people in Judah were beginning to question their current plight. The nation had paid a penalty for its sins by being captured and exiled by the Babylonians. The people had returned to Judah to a grim situation and had struggled mightily to serve Yahweh correctly and to keep Yahweh's laws. But things were not getting better; in fact on many occasions the community suffered at the hands of neighboring peoples and marauding armies as they passed through the land. In this setting the questions of the speculative wisdom thinkers and their answers to the situation became very important for the community of Jewish people in Judah. At the same time, therefore, the practical wisdom collected from the past also became more popular and emphasized in a way not heretofore acknowledged. For example, the book of Proverbs, which contains at least seven collections of practical wisdom sayings, was edited and redacted in this period. And to speak to the continuing problems of the community, the books of Job and Ecclesiastes appeared.

Mashal

In order to present the teachings of this movement a literary device known as *mashal* was developed. This Hebrew word designates the literary vehicle which carried the wisdom teaching, originally a short proverb. The word implies a *comparison*. For example, a saying would be given which presented a point or made a statement, and the hearer or reader was thereby challenged to make a comparison of that teaching with his or her own situation. As one could readily guess, most of these teachings in the earliest times were delivered as poetry. The specific forms of the teaching, however, could take various shapes: there were short pithy sayings, riddles, proverbs, parables, allegories, fables, and later on short stories. All of these were designed to present teachings in such a way that the hearers could understand the points made and apply these points in their lives or in appropriate situations.

Another dimension to the wisdom teaching in Israel involved the use of the popular device of *hyperbole*, i.e., teaching by exaggeration. Parents today use this device in attempts to teach their children right from wrong or to distinguish between safe and unsafe modes of behavior. All stoves are not always hot, but to teach a small child to avoid danger the parent may exaggerate by telling the child that all stoves are hot to emphasize that point. Hyperbole was a standard component in wisdom teaching. Unfortunately many persons today are not aware of this element in biblical teachings and become very disturbed when they discover hyperbole in certain teachings yet feel that they must take such teachings literally. For example, in the story of Jesus and the rich young man (cf. Mark 10:17–31 and parallels) Jesus tells the man to sell all he has and give it to the poor. There have been some well-known examples of persons who have taken this teaching literally. The truth is that Jesus was using hyperbole which was not intended to be taken literally, but rather to make a point. If one is aware of such methods of teaching, the interpreter is not going to be led astray into false notions and unnecessary actions.

Wisdom Stories

Another aspect in the development of the wisdom traditions in post-exilic Judaism was the use of longer stories to discuss ideas and issues, to address problems facing the community, and to offer suggestions for solutions to those problems. As already noted, the oldest wisdom traditions consisted of short sayings and proverbial expressions, but as more sophisticated development came about, longer stories began to be a major element in wisdom teachings. Numerous books in the Old Testament (and also many in the Apocrypha, a collection of intertestamental writings which are not generally accepted as authoritative by Protestant Christians) fall into this category: Job, Jonah, Ruth, and Esther. It is important to recognize these writings as wisdom stories because there is a difference in interpreting certain implications in a *story* and those same implications in a factual account.

For example, the book of Job is a story which attempts to speak to the post-exilic Jewish community in times of despair and frustration. The author used an ancient motif, that of a righteous sufferer (a motif that can also be found in ancient Egyptian and Babylonian wisdom), as the focal point to wrestle with the accepted religious understandings of the time (i.e., Deuteronomic) with regard to suffering, especially that which was interpreted as unwarranted and unwanted. The story of Job is set in the context of a wager between God and Satan (who is a member of the court of Yahweh here) with regard to whether Job would be a faithful religious person if God did not reward him for doing right. Satan argued that if Job did not have good fortune, that he would curse God. With that, the bet was on. Now it is certainly understandable for God to "roll the dice" with someone's life in a capricious manner in a story; it is quite another to believe that God carries out such capriciousness in real life. Such an idea would be quite out of character for God as depicted in the remainder of the biblical literature. If the interpreter recognizes that the story of Job is a wisdom story, however, that problem no longer exists.

Jonah

These longer wisdom stories, then, served numerous purposes in speaking to various problems which the community was experiencing in the post-exilic period. Perhaps the story of Jonah could serve to illustrate this point. The book of Jonah is found among the prophetic books, but it is not a collection of the sayings of a prophet, Jonah, as the other prophetic books are. Rather, it is a wisdom story written in the post-exilic era to illustrate a point which needed to be made to the people of that time. In those harsh years of the post-exilic era, the Jewish people in Judah were having to struggle long and hard simply to survive. Some of their leaders (Nehemiah and Ezra) had encouraged them to become a rather closed society in order to preserve themselves, their traditions, and their integrity. They were encouraged to dissociate themselves from all outsiders, to divorce any non-Jews to whom they were married, to expel these persons and any children born to them from the community, and thus to ensure their purity. These were extreme measures, but the problem here was one of survival, and survival sometimes calls for radical measures.

Not all persons agreed, however, with this strict exclusivistic approach. Some felt that the descendants of Abraham had been called to make God known to the world and that this goal could not be accomplished by building a wall around themselves. They were much more in line with the teaching of Isaiah 40—55 which emphasized that the nation of Israel was to be a "light to the nations" (cf. Isa. 42:6; 49:6). In an attempt to counter the excessive exclusivism of those times, therefore, some religious thinkers used the longer wisdom story form to lift up ideas in an effort to break through some of the more narrow teachings being espoused. Jonah, Ruth, and probably Esther fall into this category. The book of Jonah contains not only a marvelous story but a pointed message as well, a message which challenged the hearers or readers to make a comparison between Jonah and themselves.

The story is filled with typical wisdom motifs. God "appoints" almost everything in the book even down to a worm which eats a plant and kills it. Exaggeration is quite frequent, especially in the way the characters are drawn and the settings are described. For example, Nineveh was so large that it would take three days to walk across it! There is also the clear invitation for the community to look at Jonah and draw a comparison with itself.

Jonah was called to go preach to Nineveh, the great city of the hated Assyrians, but instead the prophet booked passage on a ship headed for Spain, the farthest point in the opposite direction. There is a great deal of irony in the story, especially the contrast between Jonah's feelings for others and the pagan sailors who risked their lives to save Jonah, a stranger to whom they owed nothing. Jonah was finally thrown overboard and swallowed by a great fish specially prepared by God for the purpose. The argument about whether the fish was real is really a bit superfluous since the meaning of the book is the same whether the fish was real or represents the Babylonian captivity of the Judean people.

The fish deposited Jonah on the dry land, and Jonah was given a second chance to respond positively to the call of God. He then went to Nineveh, preached to them, and told them that God's judgment was about to come upon them because of their sins. Whereupon the people repented of their sins, and God forgave them, putting aside the judgment. At this point Jonah stalked off, angry, asking to die. Interestingly enough Jonah remained close by to see if perhaps the judgment would come anyway. There are many fascinating tidbits in the story which cannot be cited fully here, but the greatest and most telling parts of the story are found in the contrast between Jonah's comment to God about Nineveh when Yahweh forgave them and

God's comment to Jonah explaining why the forgiveness was appropriate.

Jonah says: "That is why I made haste to flee to Tarshish; for I knew that thou art a gracious God and merciful, slow to anger, and abounding in steadfast love, and repentest of evil" (4:2). God says of Nineveh: "And should not I pity Nineveh, that great city, in which there are more than a hundred and twenty thousand persons who do not know their right hand from their left, and also much cattle?" (4:11). With those words from the lips of God, the book of Jonah abruptly concludes.

The story is a fascinating one and challenges the reader or hearer to make comparisons between Jonah's activities and attitudes and one's own. There is also the distinct likelihood that the original intent of the story was to cause the Hebrew people to compare themselves with Jonah. They had been called to make the name of their God known in all the world. They had failed to do this and had suffered the destruction of their nation and the Exile of the people in Babylonia. Now they had been given a second chance to fulfill their mission to the world. Why were they not doing this? Was it because of fear of failure or persecution, or the like? Or was it because they simply did not care and did not want the peoples of the world to have access to the mercies and graces of this God, Yahweh? The story of Jonah certainly parallels this history and raises those exact questions. As another wisdom teacher once said, "The one who has ears to hear, let that person hear."

Wisdom Teachers

The book of Jonah is only one example of the longer wisdom stories which became so popular in the post-exilic period. There were also wisdom teachers who gathered disciples around them and dispensed wise sayings and raised questions about life and religion. One of these was the person whose sayings are recorded in the book of Ecclesiastes. Called Qoheleth (pronounced Ko-hél-eth) this teacher wondered about life and whether it had any meaning or purpose. Another similar wisdom teacher was Joshua ben Sirach who probably had a wisdom "school" in Jerusalem about 200 B.C. His sayings are closer to the proverbial type and are recorded in the apocryphal book known as the Wisdom of Ben Sirach or Ecclesiasticus. Such thinkers also came to be great rabbis who attempted to interpret the Torah and had disciples (i.e., learners) around them. Two very famous such rabbis in Judaism at the turn of the eras were Hillel and Shammai.

For students of the biblical writings, however, the most famous such wisdom teacher was Jesus of Nazareth. According to the Synoptic Gospels (i.e., Matthew, Mark, and Luke) Jesus gathered disciples, taught them about life and religion, and used the basic teaching method of the wisdom traditions, namely short pithy sayings, parables, and perhaps a few allegories, interspersed with a healthy dose of hyperbole. For Christians, understanding Jesus' teachings properly is crucial.

At this point it is necessary to define what a parable is since so many of Jesus' teachings were delivered in that form. A parable is a wisdom teaching tool, basically a story taken from life as it is commonly observed to draw a comparison and make a point. The key to proper interpretation of a parable is to remember that a parable has basically only *one* point to make. The interpreter must be very careful not to take incidental details from the parable (which may be only descriptive "window dressing" to enhance the story) and make theological dogmas of them. Nor should the interpreter draw conclusions from the stories which were not intended.

For example, in Jesus' parable of the hidden treasure (cf. Matt. 13:44) a person finds a treasure in a field, sells all he has to buy the field in order to possess the treasure. The clear teaching here is simple: the kingdom of God is worth all that one has; its value transcends anything else one may have. Give up everything in order to enter the kingdom. Unfortunately, however, some have used this parable as a justification for questionable moral behavior in business dealings. They argue that Jesus in telling the story condones the practice of cheating people out of treasure if others are not aware of its value. Such nonsense! This is not at all implied in the parable. The basic point was made; no more should be "read out of" the story than that.

Another problem also arises frequently in interpreting the parables of Jesus. This lies in the tendency many have (especially preachers) to make allegories of the parables. An allegory is also a wisdom teaching device, but in an allegory each detail of the story is understood to have a hidden meaning. A few allegories are included among Jesus' teachings, but interestingly enough all of them are already explained (cf. Matt. 13:24–30, 36–43). The modern interpreter should not take parables and make allegories of them. The most abused parable at this point is probably the parable of the Good Samaritan. Here one of Jesus' questioners asked, "Who is my neighbor?" To respond to that question Jesus told the story of the Samaritan who helped a person who was in need (cf. Luke 10:29–37). Jesus' reply in the parable seems to be very clear: anyone in need is your neighbor.

Many sermons preached on this text ignore the fact that it is a parable and the clear teaching which it enunciates. For example, the man who was beaten and robbed has been interpreted as "everyman" and the road as "the road of life." Interesting meanings have been given to the thieves, the Samaritan, the oil, the donkey, the inn, the two pence, etc. When all this is done, it can sound very authentic. Unfortunately such interpretations are fanciful and miss the meaning of the parable.

Hyperbole

Another point where Jesus' wisdom teachings have been misunderstood lies in the fact that modern interpreters fail to note the use of hyperbole. Christians have been so conditioned to accept Jesus' teachings as definitive for their faith that they have tended to literalize those teachings. If one understands the wisdom method, however, such misunderstandings will have less opportunity to lead people astray as they seek to understand Jesus' teachings properly.

"If your right eye causes you to sin, pluck it out and throw it away;. . . . And if your right hand causes you to sin, cut it off and throw it away" (Matt. 5:29–30; cf. also Mark 9:43–48). It becomes rather clear by simple observation that no one (except perhaps the mentally disturbed) takes this directive by Jesus literally. And rightly so, for it is obvious that here is an example of the use of hyperbole in Jesus' teaching. There are, however, many other places where hyperbole was used in Jesus' teachings but where many modern interpreters have missed that point. Even well-meaning persons have misunderstood Jesus' meaning rather badly on numerous occasions.

A few examples will have to suffice for illustrative purposes. In Matthew's collection of Jesus' teachings in the Sermon on the Mount (Matt. 5—7), most of these teachings are set forth as wisdom sayings which include a healthy dose of hyperbole. Yet many persons have tried to absolutize all these teachings and have made a new legalism of them, something that Jesus actually came to abolish. One example can be found in the sayings where Jesus is speaking to the question of how best to get along in this world with people who are not committed to the same set of values as Christians, people who are by Jesus' directive atypical of the world and its attitudes. This passage is found in Matthew 5:38–42. The basic meaning of this passage lies in the emphasis upon the members of God's kingdom doing their best to break the cycle of vengeance and not giving people cause for further retaliation. The idea is to bend with "pushy people" in order to help soothe troubled waters and establish conditions which could lead to situations where people can be, at least, tranquil with each other. These sayings do *not*, however, go so far as to teach a doctrine of pacifism, even though many have attempted to found such a teaching upon them.

One of the most rigidly held legalisms in the entire history of the Christian church has been in the area of divorce. The basic teaching dealing with that issue is found in Mark 10:2–9, which culminates in the saying, "What therefore God has joined together, let not man put asunder." This saying has been taken as an absolute teaching to be understood literally. This is, of course, one way to understand the teaching, but it seems odd that Jesus who came to abolish legalisms would establish a new one, and only this one. It is also odd that this saying which is a typical wisdom teaching would be taken in such a legalistic manner.

To understand this saying better perhaps it would be helpful to present some of the background for the episode. The Torah had stated that a husband could divorce his wife for doing something "indecent" (cf. Deut. 24:1–4). The wife had no right of divorce under Jewish law. At the time of Jesus a great debate was raging among the rabbinic schools over the correct interpretation of that phrase from Deuteronomy, i.e., "some indecency." One group argued that "some indecency" could be anything from adultery to serving a meal the husband did not like to getting old and therefore physically less attractive than a younger woman. The other group argued that the phrase must refer to something exceedingly significant such as adultery. In the attempt to catch Jesus in some sort of legal slip or to alienate Jesus from certain groups of people within Judaism, some religious leaders used a series of "trick questions" to entangle and embarrass him, according to Mark. This question about divorce was one of these "entrapment" attempts.

The basic answer that Jesus gave to the question of divorce was not one which addressed the negativity of divorce but rather the positive aspects of what a real marriage is supposed to be. Jesus argued that God's purpose was for two people to become one. In such a situation, by definition, there could be no possibility for divorce. Obviously this is a saying using hyperbole to emphasize the importance of marriage. Nowhere did Jesus say that the old law was wrong; what was wrong, according to the implication of the passage, was the preoccupation of those who wanted to find ways to use the law for their own selfish purposes without regard to the intended state of marriage or the rights and needs of the wives affected by these rationalizations. Preoccupation with ways to interpret the law to encourage divorce for selfish purposes was to be deplored. What is emphasized in this teaching is the importance of marriage. A proper understanding of what marriage is seems to be the focus, not divorce. In fact the definition of marriage given here precludes divorce. If there is a question to be raised about the teaching with regard to the overall problem, it may be something like this: if two people have not become one, is there a marriage in existence at all? If not, even if two people are legally wed, are they really *married*? Here is a teaching which needs to be re-examined in the light of the background of the times and in accordance with the wisdom genre Jesus employed. Is it possible that a legalism about divorce has been created where none was intended?

Perhaps one other illustration will suffice to make the point that Jesus frequently used hyperbole. In the Sermon on the Mount a series of sayings called the "Antitheses" is attributed to Jesus. They begin, "You have heard that it was said. . . . But I say to you. . . ." (cf. Matt. 5:21–48). In these contrasts between the external interpretations of the law and Jesus' clear understanding that there is an underlying meaning which is more important, there is a specific appeal to look for the intent of the law's teachings. It is not enough simply not to kill; one must not hate. Other illustrations are cited also to emphasize the point. Some people, however, have taken these teachings so literally that they have become guilt-ridden and self-demeaning because of their "evil thoughts." It is true that Jesus places the initial blame for external acts of sin on the inner disposition of the person. This inner disposition, however, is understood as an active, willing, preoccupied disposition which leads to explicit action, not simply passing thoughts. If this wisdom method of teaching can be understood by modern interpreters, great relief can be given those who have misinterpreted these sayings so literally and have carried so much guilt.

Some, however, argue on the other extreme (especially on the teaching about adultery) that if it is just as bad to think an evil thought as to do it, why not enjoy the sin fully! Such an interpretation is taking a literal meaning of the text too far in the other direction. What the interpreter must learn to do is to recognize the wisdom teachings and their peculiarities in order to interpret Jesus' teachings properly. Not all of Jesus' teachings are of the wisdom type, but so many are that one must understand this teaching procedure to interpret Jesus' teachings correctly.

Wisdom teaching became a major part of Israel's religious heritage, especially developing in the post-exilic period. Because this movement gave such practical guidance to persons trying to survive in this world and because the later speculative wisdom attempted to make sense of the world when nothing seemed to make any sense, wisdom grew very popular with the people and has survived even to this day!

Suggestions for Further Study

Crenshaw, James L. *Old Testament Wisdom: An Introduction*. Atlanta: John Knox Press, 1981.

Efird, James M. *Biblical Books of Wisdom.* Valley Forge, Pa.: Judson Press, 1983.

Fuerst, Wesley J. *The Books of Ruth, Esther, Ecclesiastes, The Song of Songs, Lamentations.* Cambridge: Cambridge University Press, 1975.

Habel, Norman C. *The Book of Job.* Cambridge: Cambridge University Press, 1975.

Whybray, R. N. *The Book of Proverbs.* Cambridge: Cambridge University Press, 1972.

VI

How to Interpret Apocalyptic Literature

Of all the different literary types found in the biblical materials none has been so grievously misunderstood as that known as apocalyptic. This literary phenomenon developed in the post-exilic age within Judaism against the backdrop of Persian thought and the attempt to explain the harsh realities which the community in Judah was experiencing. What began as a "thought pattern" then developed a literary style which served as a vehicle for the apocalyptic message.

Two basic ideas in Persian thought slipped over into Hebraic thinking in the post-exilic period when Judah was under the domination of the Persians. The Persians believed that there were two forces in the universe, good and evil, and that these forces were locked in a life and death struggle for superiority and ultimate victory. While this battle was being waged at the cosmic level of the universe, all creation, especially the world in which humans live, was directly involved. In this struggle sometimes good had the upper hand; sometimes good and evil were virtually "even"; and at other moments the forces of evil gained the upper hand. When this occurred those who were on the side of good (God) suffered and suffered intensely. The Persians believed that a great final battle would end the world as it is now known. The forces of good would win and the forces of evil would be defeated in a decisive manner.

Since the Jews believed Yahweh was the only "eternal" being and supreme over evil, these ideas could not be accepted into Jewish thought as they were, but rather they were modified somewhat and used to interpret the "times" which the Jewish people were experiencing. One can readily see how this type of thinking would be very appropriate for a group of people who were trying their best to be devoted to God but continued to experience harsh times. Why this was happening could then be understood as part of a much larger conflict, and these people could find some comfort in the belief that even though they were suffering, at least they were on the right side. In fact, the very presence of suffering in their lives was a reminder to them that they were doing what God wanted them to do. This thinking was far different from the old Deuteronomic theology and the basic premise of practical wisdom teaching, but it explained for that time and place why evil continued to plague the people's existence.

Several related matters must be mentioned in connection with this thought pattern. Against the backdrop of apocalyptic ideology there developed in Jewish thought a highly complex hierarchy of angels and demons, supernatural beings which were part of the cosmic struggle between good and evil. Since the beings which were allied with good had a leader, namely God, it stood to reason that the forces of evil must also have a leader. This one who came to be understood as the epitome of evil was known as Satan. Several other names were used in the Jewish writings of the period (the late post-exilic period, about 250 B.C. and after), namely Belial, Beelzebub, Asmodeus, the devil, and Satan. The last mentioned name finally "won out" over the others, perhaps because that figure is mentioned in the Old Testament writings (Job, Zechariah, and Chronicles). Interestingly enough Satan in these documents was not the leader of the forces of evil; rather he was a servant in the court of God whose basic duty it was to report to God the foibles of human beings, hence the name *Satan*, the Accuser.

Further, the idea of conflict between the forces of good and evil and the concept of a great confrontation in which evil would be defeated were modified somewhat in Jewish thought. Here the historicizing aspect of the Hebrew mind came to bear upon these Persian ideas with the result that the great battle was seen as being fought primarily within the sphere of human history. Jewish thinking emphasized the idea that there were those periods of time when the forces of evil would gain the upper hand in human history, and in such times the good people, i.e., those faithful to God, would suffer intense persecution. In such periods the idea emerged that history (usually *present* history) was divided into two ages, a present evil age totally dominated by the powers of evil and for which there was no real hope, and a coming new age which would be brought about by the intervention of God (or God's representative) in which the evil would be removed and the persecution of God's people would cease. The descriptions of these "new ages" (for each apocalyptic work described one) varied from writer to writer. In some the older Persian idea of a "last" judgment was used, but in many the new age took other forms and shapes. For example, in the two biblical apocalyptic books (Daniel, especially chapters 7—12, and Revelation) the new age is simply the continuation of the historical order as now known but with the persecution removed.

The two basic ideas connected with apocalyptic thought, therefore, are the struggle between good and evil and the idea of the two ages, a present evil age and a better age to come soon. Such thinking would find its natural historical context, then, in periods of persecution or despair, exactly what was happening to the Jewish people in Judah during the post-exilic times. In order to enunciate these basic ideas and to speak dramatically to the people who were experiencing persecution, apocalyptic thinkers developed a highly symbolic literary style to convey their messages of hope in the midst of cruel circumstances. This development was probably the result of the fact that these writers wished to make certain that the persecuted people understood clearly the magnitude of the events they were experiencing and what lay behind their persecution and the full implications of any decision on their part to succumb to the pressures of those harsh times and to "go over" to the side of evil. What they had dedicated their lives to—good, truth, light, God—was of far more lasting value than the commitment of those on the "other" side— evil, lies, darkness, Satan. The basic message of the apocalyptic writers then was to urge the people not to forsake those things which are lasting and eternal for the sake of momentary relief.

Dramatic Symbolism

The apocalyptic literary style came to be filled with dramatic symbolism. Usually the whole scene was set in the context of a vision or a series of visions told with exaggerated symbols. Animals usually represented nations. Horns represented either power or a person who exercised power (namely a ruler). Colors were important, especially white (victory), red (war), and black (the lack of something—peace, food, health, etc.). Numbers were quite frequently used and usually with specific connotations. Three stood for the "spirit" world; four for the created order; seven represented completeness usually in the sense of "maturity" or fullness; ten represented completeness usually in the sense of a completed number of the totality of whatever was designated. Twelve in Jewish and Christian apocalyptic stood for the people of God. The apocalyptic writers liked to "manipulate" numbers in that they would square or cube them (to intensify the meaning) and sometimes would even multiply two different numbers together to symbolize and dramatize some point being made. For example, the fascinating number found in the book of Revelation, 144,000, of which so much (too much in fact) has been made is 12 squared times 10 cubed. If one can learn to think symbolically as these persons did, the mystery is really removed. The number 12, representing the people of God, and the number 10, representing completeness (in the sense of a unit), are combined here to represent the total number of the people of God. In apocalyptic one cannot count numbers in a literal manner.

One other number is frequently used in apocalyptic writings; this is the number 3½. It takes different forms, e.g., "a time, two times, and half a time," forty-two months (3½ years), one thousand two hundred and sixty days, etc., but the idea remains the same. This represented the designated period that God "allowed" evil to run its course, during which time the people of God endured suffering and persecution. It was to be a "short" period, and the faithfulness of God's people could both shorten the time and play a part in the ultimate victory that God would surely win over these evil forces.

In addition to the weird symbols and use of exaggerated figures, there seems to have been in each apocalyptic writing a "historical survey" told in highly symbolic language which rehearsed the movement of history from some place in the past to the present time of evil and persecution. Some apocalyptic works contained more than one of these surveys. Usually these historical descriptions ranged over a long period of history because the one who supposedly "saw"

the vision was an ancient worthy of the past. Most apocalyptic writings were pseudonymous, a common literary practice among the
Jewish people at this particular moment of history. The interesting
aspect about the weird scenes is that they are quite frequently explained to the one who saw them by a heavenly companion or angel.
Not every aspect of the vision was identified (probably because a
great deal of apocalyptic imagery was only intended to be "window
dressing" to enhance the dramatic impact of the scene), but those
elements which the author wanted especially not to be misunderstood were clearly explained.

Earlier commentators on apocalyptic writings often argued that
the symbolism of these documents resulted from the fact that the
persecuted people did not dare proclaim their messages in such a
way that the persecutors would understand them. The persecuted
people developed, therefore, this cryptic form of writing to com-
municate with each other while leaving the persecutor in the dark. If
one reads these works carefully, however, there is no way that the
message could be misunderstood even by the persecutors. Assuming
that the persecutors could read, there is then no real attempt to hide
the message from them. The idea that this symbolism was used to
serve as a camouflage simply does not fit the facts. Probably the
symbolism was developed for its dramatic impact, to serve as a vehicle for depicting the hideous nature of evil and its cohorts and the
even greater power of the only One who would bring evil to its just
deserts, namely God. The truth is that the persecutors did not really
care what these writings said. The apocalyptic writers were not advocating armed rebellion, only passive resistance, which basically
took the form of refusing to worship a king or other gods. These
oppressed people were really powerless; the persecutors probably
thought that these books might even help to keep these people more
passive. The message of each apocalyptic work was that God would
execute the vengeance on evil and those who allied themselves
with evil.

To interpret apocalyptic literature properly, therefore, one must
be aware of these thought patterns and the literary genre which conveyed them to people under persecution and in evil times. Apocalyptic is not easy for modern persons to understand because this type of

thinking and these types of symbols are to a certain degree foreign to our minds. If one can recognize these writings as basically symbolic, however, half the battle is already won. The other prerequisite for interpreting apocalyptic properly is to understand and know something about the historical circumstances which called forth the apocalyptic writing being considered. This is absolutely crucial, and in most instances these circumstances can be known. The reader of ancient apocalyptic works today, therefore, must remember that these thought patterns and literary symbolism were very popular in that period of history. Therefore, the best way to understand the writing properly is to attempt to place oneself in that historical setting and understand the document as the first hearers (or readers) would have understood it. After all, these books were originally written for their own time and place; if we are to understand them properly we must begin there also.

Popular Misinterpretations of Biblical Apocalyptic

Unfortunately there have been attempts to make something of these works which they were never intended to be—namely timetables for the end of the world. Apocalyptic literature and thought flourished from about 200 B.C. to A.D. 100; after that time the literary genre died out and so too did a proper understanding of what these documents really said and meant. Early in the Christian era (i.e., after A.D. 100) some attempted to make of Revelation (and to a lesser degree, Daniel) a timetable for the return of Jesus. Such attempts were understood to be false and an improper use of the document by the majority of the early Christian leaders. Because of such misusages of the book by some persons, the book of Revelation was only grudingly and reluctantly admitted into the canon of the New Testament by the church.

Through the years the book of Revelation was mainly ignored by the majority of the church because few, if any, really understood how to interpret the book properly. It remained, however, a happy hunting ground for many sincere but misguided persons.

One of the most popular current interpretations of the book of Revelation is a direct outgrowth of a movement that began in the early nineteenth century. The driving force behind this interpretative method was a man named John Nelson Darby, an Irishman born in England who gave up a career in law to become a priest of the Church of England. While recovering from a physical ailment, he had some sort of religious experience in 1827. The recuperative process took almost two years and during this time he became preoccupied with the idea of the end of the world and the details of Jesus' return. Using the book of Revelation primarily at first, he began to find hidden clues in the symbols which he believed enabled him to calculate the time, place, and circumstances of this momentous event.

In the course of his life he attracted some followers who used his presuppositions and brought them to bear on the interpretation of the biblical texts. Many biblical materials were added to this interpretative method—primarily Daniel, some of Jesus' teachings, some of Paul's teachings, and later even the teachings of the prophets. It is not the purpose here to recite all the steps of this interpretative development, but Darby's views as they had been expanded were popularly disseminated in this country by the famous *Scofield Reference Bible* which first appeared in the early part of this century. It is noted for the system of teaching which is commonly known as dispensationalism. The text of this Bible was the King James Version with notes by Cyrus I. Scofield, a disciple of Darby, using Darby's interpretative method which by this time had many additional elements added to it both in terms of content and method. The popular manifestation of the method presently current in our society is found in the work of Hal Lindsey, *The Late, Great Planet Earth*, and numerous other books, tapes, and records.

This interpretative method has not been present in the church "forever" as some have claimed. Rather it is a relatively new interpretative movement which uses certain presuppositions which it imposes upon the biblical materials in an attempt to discover when the end of the world and the return of Jesus are going to occur. Usually the time is understood as "almost here," and identifications are constantly made from the biblical texts to personalities and events in current history. Such identifications have been made and the time seen as "now" for more than 150 years.

One cannot but wonder why after 150 years of such speculation, all of which has turned out to be false and untrue (except what is being currently predicted), that persons would not ask a simple question: if these identifications and speculations about the "end" have been wrong for 150 years, could it not be possible that this method of interpretation is wrong? And could it be that these texts were not intended to be used in such a manner and for such a purpose? So far, the advocates of this position have simply changed the historical identifications as the years continue to roll by, frequently adding "new" insights which heretofore they had "overlooked." (One of the most famous of these currently in vogue has to do with the creation of the state of Israel in 1948, and many present calculations have been made with regard to this event.) The most obvious answer to the question as to why none of these schemes or predictions has come to pass, however, is that these texts were never intended to be understood in such a way. Careful study of the books themselves demonstrates clearly that this is true, and careful study will also clarify how one can understand these texts properly.

Daniel

The best way to counter such improper interpretations is to examine several of the key passages in Daniel and Revelation to ascertain exactly what they meant when originally written. One passage, which illustrates the apocalyptic use of symbols and images, the vision motif, the historical survey, and the angelic interpreter, can be found in Daniel 8. Here the reader finds Daniel having a vision in which he saw a ram with two horns, one longer than the other. The ram ran to the west and north and south. This was a powerful figure. But suddenly there came from the west another figure, a he-goat with a huge horn between his eyes. This beast moved so fast that it appeared not even to touch the ground. These two engaged in battle with the he-goat destroying the ram. Then the great horn of the he-goat was broken, and in its place there arose four smaller horns. Out of one of these emerged a "little horn" which grew great "toward the glorious land." This "little horn" took away the continual burnt offerings, overthrew the sanctuary, and suppressed the "truth." Daniel was told that this sacrilege would go on for "two thousand and three hundred evenings and mornings."

Here is a mysterious and strange passage. If one presupposes that this is a prediction in cryptic form of events that are happening or about to happen in the twentieth century, then the door is open for any and all types of applications to modern persons or nations or events. If one understands the nature of apocalyptic literature and the historical setting in which this book was written, however, the meaning of the passage becomes rather clear.

During the early post-exilic period the Jewish people in Judah were under the dominion of the Persian government, one of the greatest of all nations to that point in history. This empire stretched to the west, north, and south from its base in old Persia (basically what is modern Iran). In the fourth century B.C. Alexander the Great of Macedonia invaded this part of the world, broke the might of the Persian Empire in 331 B.C., and went on to India. Supposedly he wept because there were no more worlds to conquer. At the height of his power he died (323 B.C.), whereupon his generals began to fight for succession to control Alexander's empire. After the smoke of the battles had cleared, the empire had been divided into four smaller units. Only two concerned the Jewish people in Judah, however: the Ptolemaic Empire in Egypt and the Seleucid Empire in old Persia reaching into northern Palestine.

At first the Jewish people were under the authority of the Ptolemies in Egypt. As one could guess, however, the Ptolemies and the Seleucids fought over control of southern Palestine. Finally in 198 B.C. the Ptolemies gave control of that area to the Seleucids. Shortly thereafter, the Seleucid king, Antiochus IV called Epiphanes (i.e., "God manifest"), had trouble with the Jewish people. Realizing that his troubles were the result of their religion, he simply proscribed Judaism, i.e., it became illegal to be a Jew, to keep the dietary laws, to circumcise a male child on the eighth day, to have a copy of the Torah, etc. Antiochus made the temple in Jerusalem into a shrine for the Greek god, Zeus, and erected there a statue of Zeus (which many said bore a striking resemblance to Antiochus). He even had pigs sacrificed on the altar of Yahweh. Naturally, there was conflict over this state of affairs.

During this time the book of Daniel was written, to speak to the Jewish people in this period of persecution. The first six chapters of

Daniel are basically wisdom stories told to bolster the faith and re-solve of these people who were experiencing this horrible tragedy. The last six chapters are written in the apocalyptic style, of which chapter 8 is a standard specimen.

Here the interpreter finds the typical apocalyptic motif, a vision, in which Daniel sees weird figures and wonders what it all means. If one can recall that such scenes are in apocalyptic "historical sur-veys," and if one knows the history of that period, there is really no mystery to this bizarre scene. The ram with the two horns, one of which was larger (the second one), represents the Median-Persian Empire which became one of the greatest nations the world up to that time had ever known. It expanded from its base in Persia to the west, north, and south. The he-goat from the west with the single huge horn between its eyes represents the Greeks, precisely the Macedonian armies under the command of Alexander the Great. The Greeks defeated the Persians and caused the death of that empire. At the height of his power, however, Alexander died, i.e., "the great horn was broken," and after his generals fought for the spoils of the kingdom, there emerged four separate and smaller kingdoms.

Out of one of these kingdoms arose another king (a little horn) who captured the "glorious land" (Palestine) and proscribed the true religion. This "little horn" obviously refers to Antiochus IV who was at that time persecuting the people of God. After a short period (3½ years) the true religion would be reinstated. Now if the modern reader is unconvinced by these identifications from the historical data known about those times, there is yet another source of information which cannot be doubted. That source is the text of Daniel itself! If one will go on to read 8:18–25, there is absolutely no question that these are the identifications which the inspired author of Daniel intended.

There is a clear warning here for any interpreter of the biblical materials: it is to be honest with the biblical text even if one wishes to disagree with it. If one wishes to deny the plain meaning of the biblical text itself and to accept fanciful speculation about contem-porary people and nations, one may do so only to the extent that it is clearly understood that this is not the meaning of the biblical text.

One must be honest at this point and admit that such fanciful interpretation falls into the category of speculation, sometimes even fiction, no more, no less.

The Beast in Revelation

Two similar passages in the book of Revelation are also much abused in the same way: chapters 13 and 17. In chapter 13 one finds a beast which rises from the sea with seven heads, one of which has a mortal wound which has healed. This beast persecutes the people of God and enlists the aid of a lamb beast to assist in that process. Together they deny the people allied with God the right to buy or sell, i.e., to participate normally in the ongoing life of the state. Everyone has to be "marked" with the number of the beast (which the reader is told is a "man's name"). This number in some early Greek copies of the New Testament reads 666; in other early copies and versions, however, the number is 616. The question to be answered in understanding this text is whether one person can be found whose identity will explain the numbers and the curious reference to the "head with the mortal wound which was healed."

In that period of history most cultures counted by means of their alphabet; a lingering example of this phenomenon is represented in our culture by the occasional use of Roman numerals. When letters are used as numerals, this means that every person's name also has a number. Quite frequently numerical designations for people were utilized in ancient society. For example, on the walls of Pompeii someone had written a note, "I love her whose number is 545." This illustrates that society then was familiar with this device, the technical term for which is *gematria*.

The book of Revelation was written, according to the oldest traditions and in the opinion of the vast majority of New Testament scholars, during the time of the Roman emperor Domitian, who ruled A.D. 81–96. Most Roman emperors were voted divine status by the Roman senate upon death; but a few of these rulers wanted to be worshiped as a god during their lifetimes. Domitian was one of these. In the province of Asia Minor (what is now modern Turkey) Domitian encouraged, even demanded, the worship of himself as a god and of Roma, the patron goddess of the Roman state. Those persons who would not burn incense to the statue of the emperor were looked upon as enemies of Rome. Christians in the area were, naturally, in a dilemma. To them the homage being demanded by Domitian belonged only to God and to Jesus the Christ; to burn the incense was an act of idolatry and apostasy. They refused to do this, and therefore they were persecuted. If the interpreter is familiar with the history of those early years of the Christian movement, it becomes clear that there were two types of persecution the members of this new religious movement experienced: local and sporadic persecution, and persecution at the hands of the Roman government. There was no empire-wide persecution of Christians by Rome until A.D. 250, but periodically emperors or governmental authorities did harass and even kill these people in isolated instances. The first of these governmental persecutions occurred under the emperor Nero A.D. 64–66. Nero had a part of Rome burned so that he could rebuild it as he wished, but politically speaking this act backfired on him. He had to find a scapegoat, and he found it in this new group called Christians. In that bitter time tradition indicates that both Peter and Paul along with many others were killed. Remembering the tendency to concretize all subsequent portions of a movement in the initiator of the movement (cf. Moses and the law, David and psalms, Solomon and wisdom), one should not be surprised to find that any time a Roman emperor persecuted the Christians they would understand this as the reappearance of Nero or "Nero reborn."

Since Domitian was at that time persecuting the Christians in Asia Minor, the people experiencing those harsh times thought that Nero had returned. Since heads on beasts in apocalyptic literature usually represented rulers, the reference to a head which had a mortal wound which had healed could very easily, even probably, have been intended and understood as a reference to Nero. The beast is identified as having authority over all the earth and as persecuting the people of God. There can be little question that the beast is Rome.

The problem with the numbers is harder to decipher, however, for no "man's name" in Greek really can be found which will total 666 (not to mention 616). The book of Revelation, however, has a strong Aramaic background. This leads to a possibility that the man's name may have been understood in Aramaic characters. If one puts the words, *Neron Caesar*, into Aramaic letters, the total of the name yields 666. If one writes the name as *Nero Caesar* (either way was acceptable in Aramaic), the total of the name yields 616! In other words the name and figure of Nero explains the wounded head which was healed, the number 666, and the number 616. It is clear from the text that the writer of Revelation is not predicting someone to come in the future but is describing someone and some power present *at that time*.

Fanciful explanations which interpret the beast as modern economic entities (such as the European Common Market) or a giant computer in Belgium are simply nonsense. The mark of the beast, i.e., 666, likewise has been identified as social security numbers or the universal product code on packages. The beast has been called the "antichrist" even though that term *never* appears in the book of Revelation, and it has been identified with many different persons in history such as Kaiser Wilhelm, Adolf Hitler, Benito Mussolini, Gen. Hideki Tojo, Joseph Stalin, Ho Chi Min, Henry Kissinger, the Ayatullah Khomeini, Menachem Begin, etc. Such attempts at identifying modern personalities with this figure are simply not legitimate.

A similar symbolic description is found in chapter 17. Here the reader finds a woman seated on a beast who is depicted as persecuting the saints of God. Again an explanation is given of the woman and the beast with seven heads, and again the answer comes out Rome. "The woman that you saw is the great city which has dominion over the kings of the earth" (Rev. 17:18). The woman is also described as "Babylon." Since Babylon was the first conquerer of Jerusalem in 597 and 586 B.C., all nations that conquered Jerusalem could be designated as Babylon. When the Romans sacked Jerusalem in A.D. 70, the Jewish people began to refer to Rome as Babylon, and the Christians probably picked up that designation from them (cf. also 1 Peter 5:13).

The "Last" Judgment

One last passage which deserves attention is found in Revelation 20:1—22:5. This segment is sometimes understood as the "final drama" in the saga of the world, the last judgment, and the consignment of all people to either heaven or hell. Interestingly enough very few persons have been able to make sense of this passage partly because most attempt to interpret these verses rather literally. Up to this point almost everything in the book of Revelation has been intended to be interpreted symbolically. Why not 20:1—22:5 also?

Many outlandish schemes have been concocted to interpret what these chapters are describing. In addition there are many variations even within the various schemes as to the details of the scenarios which will precede "*the end*." The most well-known and popular of these schemes goes something like this: Jesus returns and binds Satan for a thousand years; the saints then reign with Jesus on earth for a thousand years in a blissful kingdom; after this Satan is set free and a great bloody battle takes place (the battle of Armageddon); then the last judgment takes place, the world is destroyed, and all people are assigned to heaven or hell. This scheme is known as premillennial, i.e., Jesus returns before the thousand-year earthly reign. Others add all sorts of "extras" to this description such as a "rapture" (i.e., the taking up into the air of the saints at the return of Jesus), a second return of Jesus, a second rapture, periods of time such as seven years or three and one-half years in which certain specified events transpire before the millennium.

If the interpreter will read these chapters carefully, however, it will be noted that most of the items listed above are simply not there. And others have been greatly distorted and misunderstood. For example, the reign of the saints with Jesus *on the earth* is simply not taught here. The saints who have been "beheaded for their testimony to Jesus" (20:4) are not on earth; they are in heaven (cf. Rev. 6:9). This is where the "reigning" takes place. Further, there is no mention in this passage of a great battle taking place and no mention of a place called Armageddon (cf. Rev. 16:16). There is mention of every person having to face the judgment seat of God (20:12), but there is no mention that this event occurs at the same time for all people or that the world as presently known is destroyed.

Verses 21:1—22:5 describe a "new heaven and a new earth." This "new" is understood as transformed, not made from new "components." The heavenly city, Jerusalem, is not a description of heaven but a symbolic description of how the people of God will experience God's abiding presence when the "new age" comes, the new age with the persecution removed. There is mention of "death being no more," but in this book "death" has been understood as martyr's death. The "sea is no more" because the beast, which persecuted God's people, arose from the sea. These figures symbolize for God's people the triumph of God over the power and forces of evil. It is interesting to find in 21:24–27 and 22:2 that the "nations" which can be evil and which stand in need of "healing" are still around. How can that be if the world has come to an end and all people have gone to heaven or hell? Obviously that interpretation was not what the author of Revelation intended. What he is describing symbolically is a new age for God's people with the persecution removed.

Many people are greatly disappointed to learn that this is the basic meaning of the book of Revelation. They counter with, "Is that *all* there is to it?" Anyone who can say such a thing has never really experienced genuine persecution where death was a real possibility, even perhaps a probability. No one in those settings would think that the removal of persecution and the establishment of a new era with no persecution were simple matters to be shrugged off as insignificant. Those persons who saw the gates to the concentration camps of World War II swing open at the hands of the liberators would hardly have said: "Is that all?" For them a new age had indeed dawned. That persecution at least was over. The apocalyptic writers of Daniel and Revelation depicted similar situations and spoke to those beleaguered people to bolster their faith and resolve and to reassure the faithful that God was ultimately in control even if it appeared not to be so at the moment.

There are other apocalyptic teachings in the New Testament especially in the teachings of Jesus and the earlier writings of Paul. If the interpreter will remember the basic ideas of apocalyptic literature, i.e., the dualism and conflict between good and evil, the two-age motif, the essential ingredient of persecution, and the use of symbols to designate and depict all these aspects, this peculiar and often strange literature will become more meaningful and can be understood as it was intended to be understood.

Suggestions for Further Study

Beegle, Dewey M. *Prophecy and Prediction*. Ann Arbor, Mich.: Pryor Pettengill, Publisher, 1978.

Beasley-Murray, G. R. *The Book of Revelation*. London: Oliphants, 1974; reprint ed., Greenwood, S.C.: Attic Press, 1978; Grand Rapids, Mich.: Wm. B. Eerdmans Publishing Company, 1981.

Efird, James M. *Daniel and Revelation: A Study of Two Extraordinary Visions*. Valley Forge, Pa.: Judson Press, 1978.

Hammer, Raymond. *The Book of Daniel*. Cambridge: Cambridge University Press, 1976.

Russell, D. S. *Apocalyptic: Ancient and Modern*. Philadelphia: Fortress Press, 1978.

VII

How to Interpret the Gospels

When interpreters of the Bible turn to the writings known as the New Testament, they are naturally struck with the fact that all these writings revolve in one way or another around the person known as Jesus of Nazareth. It is not surprising, therefore, to find that the entire New Testament collection begins with accounts of the ministry of Jesus. What is surprising, however, is the fact that there are four different presentations of that ministry, each having its own peculiar emphases and interpretation of Jesus and Jesus' ministry. These four accounts of Jesus' ministry are called "Gospels," from the Greek word *euangelion* which means "good news."

From an examination of these documents when compared to other types of biographical accounts in the world of that time, it becomes clear that the early church or Mark (the first gospel writer) developed a new literary form to convey the church's understandings and interpretations of Jesus. This literary form became known as a "Gospel." it is obvious even to the casual reader of these works that exact biography was not the intention of the writers of the Gospels, though they used traditions which were biographical in nature. It is also clear that these documents do not presume to recite an exact account of what Jesus did or said and where he went, even though there is obviously much historical material incorporated into these accounts. What emerged in the early church was a literary genre that is similar in many respects to the historical writings already discussed. The Gospel writers used history, biography, and other types of traditions and wove these elements into a religious interpretation of Jesus of Nazareth suitable for the specific church community for which each author was writing. These Gospels are different from the other historical writings, however, in that they are concerned to interpret the events connected with a single personality rather than an entire community.

In order to interpret these writings properly, it is exceedingly important to realize that those materials which contained the traditions concerned with Jesus' life and teaching had been subjected to a developmental process before finding a final place in one or more of these four Gospels. The process of remembering, transmitting, and using these traditions is much more complex than most persons have ever imagined, and that process cannot be reconstructed with absolute certainty. Most of those who study this problem closely, however, have found that several stages were involved in the passing along of these materials which ultimately can be traced back to the actual life of Jesus. First of all, stories about Jesus and teachings of Jesus existed in oral form. These stories and teachings were obviously treasured by the members of the early Christian community and were used to speak to the needs of that community. In the process of this oral transmission (and translation from Aramaic into Greek) most of these materials were circulated in single, self-contained units called *pericopes* (a Greek word meaning something that has been "cut around"). The only exception to this general rule seems to have been the Passion narrative, i.e., the account of Jesus' suffering, which probably circulated as a longer story from the beginning. These individual units were then used and reused in the church to fit various needs and differing situations. After a while some of them appear to have been put together into short collections usually revolving around a particular theme or type of saying (cf. Mark 2:1—3:6, a series of stories about Jesus in conflict with religious authorities, or Mark 4:1–34, a collection of parables describing the kingdom of God). There is even some evidence to suggest that a large collection of the sayings of Jesus was compiled. Numerous strands of traditions about Jesus developed over a period of forty to seventy years.

Since the early church originally believed very strongly in the imminent return of Jesus, there seemed to be no real need at first to write down a story about Jesus. Eyewitnesses could relay episodes and teachings as needed. As time went by, however, a genuine need began to be felt to write a "history" of Jesus. The first generation of Christians was almost gone, and it began to be assumed that the return of Jesus had been delayed, for how long no one knew. The first of these Gospels was, therefore, written shortly after the deaths of Peter and Paul in Rome during the persecution of the Christians by Nero A.D. 64–66. According to the earliest traditions the Gospel was written about A.D. 68 by John Mark, who was a companion of Simon Peter in his travels throughout the Greco-Roman world. Tradition says that Mark wrote down what he remembered of Peter's teachings about Jesus to preserve them for the church; interestingly enough, however, the earliest tradition specifically states that the materials were *not* written down "in order." In the composition of this first portrait of Jesus, most scholars believe that Mark also used other traditions about Jesus which were known to him and which were current in the early church.

Form Criticism

The traditions about Jesus' life and teaching, therefore, had gone through several levels of development before the Gospel writers used them. If the interpreter examines several of Jesus' sayings carefully, some of the ways the early Christian community handled these units become clear. For example Mark 2:18–20 is a story of Jesus' discussing with the Pharisees why his disciples were not fasting. The answer given was in the form of a wisdom saying: "Can the wedding guests fast while the bridegroom is with them?" This response seems appropriate to the occasion and certainly fits the context of the story. In the early Christian community, however, there were serious discussions about whether the new people of God ought to fast. It is probable that most persons in the early church felt that the solution to this problem should be positive since Jesus was no longer physically present with the disciples. Therefore, to this saying of Jesus the early church *may* have added the next words, "as long as they have the bridegroom with them they cannot fast. The days will come, when the bridegroom is taken way from them, and then they will fast in that day." This saying then solved a problem which the early Christians faced, and demonstrates how they used the teachings of Jesus. Their understanding of handling and interpreting Jesus' teaching seems to have been to follow a particular teaching and draw from that teaching what appeared to them to be logical inferences. To modern persons such use of the traditions seems to presuppose a rather cavalier attitude toward sacred revelation. This is to impose our understandings upon them, however. While the early disciples reverenced deeply the stories about Jesus and the teachings of Jesus, they did not yet believe that these materials were "revelation" in the same sense as they later were understood to be. Therefore, there was a decided looseness in the handling of the materials as judged by modern standards.

Another illustration of this point can be seen by examination of another passage in Mark (2:23–28). Here Jesus and his disciples are walking through the grainfields on a Sabbath, and the disciples pluck the grain—considered work according to the interpretation of the Torah current at that time. When questioned about the disciples' action by the religious authorities, Jesus replied, "The sabbath was made for man, not man for the sabbath; so the Son of man is lord even of the sabbath." In the saying as it is presented by Mark the intention was to depict Jesus as Son of Man and thus "Lord of the Sabbath." Whatever Jesus allowed and did on the Sabbath was certainly permissible. This is the meaning of the saying as Mark uses it in his Gospel.

If the interpreter studies the background of the passage, however, several interesting things become evident. First is the fact that the term "Son of Man" could and did have various usages in the first century. It was widely used in the Old Testament to refer to "a man" or "humanity," usually in a condition of weakness. Secondly, the term could be used as another designation for "I," in much the same way that people today say "the writer" or "this speaker" when referring to themselves. Thirdly, the term was used as a title (cf. the book of Daniel where it is a collective term representing the people of God in Dan. 7:13–18; and the book of Enoch where it refers to a semidivine being through whom God intended to accomplish great things for the holy people). In the original Aramaic which Jesus spoke, the term could have been used with any one of these meanings. It is possible, then, that some of Jesus' teachings could have been misunderstood or perhaps interpreted in a different way to suit the needs of the early community.

For example, in this passage (Mark 2:27–28) the original saying could possibly have meant, "The sabbath was made for man (humanity), not man for the sabbath; so man is lord even of the sabbath." The teaching would then have been directed at the narrowness of religious legalism which would place rigid regulations above human need. A second possibility is that the original saying ended with verse 27; verse 28 would have been a confession of the church about Jesus which was added to the original saying. Further, it is possible that the saying meant, "The sabbath was made for man not man for the sabbath; so I am lord even of the sabbath." Here Jesus would have been asserting his authority over against the authority of the religious leaders. Since it is clear from a reading of the Gospels that the early church understood the term "Son of Man" to be a titular self-designation used by Jesus of himself, it is easy to understand how in some of these sayings when the term "Son of Man" was used with other nuances the church simply identified all these usages as titles. In other words the church understood in this passage (2:28) the term "Son of Man" to have been a title claimed by Jesus to demonstrate his authority over the old law. They could then appeal to a passage like this to support their claim that Jesus had transcended the old Torah and that his teachings had replaced it!

One can easily determine from this brief examination of these two passages that the study of the traditions about Jesus and Jesus' sayings can be quite fascinating and quite complicated. The methodological discipline which emerged and pioneered in this type of study is known as *form criticism*. It is not the purpose of this discussion to explore in detail all the facets of that discipline; rather it is to introduce the interpreter to the process and illustrate what types of questions and investigations the adherents of the discipline address. One can readily see that the discipline is highly speculative and should be used with caution and care, but at some points this kind of study can illuminate the teachings of Jesus and the needs of the early church in a most dramatic way. (For further discussion of the methodology consult the bibliography at the conclusion of this chapter.)

Source Criticism

A second method related to the interpretation of the Gospels is called *source criticism*. The work done in this area is similar in many ways to the type of investigation done on the Torah, though the source materials here, naturally, are of a quite different type. For many years people have realized that the first three Gospels are different from the fourth Gospel. Matthew, Mark, and Luke are similar in outline and in the presentation of Jesus' life and teachings, whereas John presents a different outline and method of teaching. It was also long believed (since the time of Augustine in the fifth century) that Matthew was the oldest of these with Mark being a condensation of Matthew. Because of the similarity of Matthew, Mark, and Luke, these three became known as the *Synoptic Gospels* because they "see together" the ministry of Jesus.

With the emergence of critical analysis of the biblical materials in the eighteenth and nineteenth centuries, closer investigation was made of these documents. A major point of interest lay in the fact that while these three are so similar in many details, they are also different. That puzzle came to be known as the "Synoptic problem"; why are these three so alike, and yet at points so different? Gradually a "solution" to the Synoptic problem emerged, based primarily on a source-critical analysis of the materials. It came to be recognized (as the oldest traditions of the church had clearly indicated) that Mark was the first of the Gospels to have been written. Careful analysis of Mark in conjunction with a study of Matthew and Luke revealed a common denominator among these three in terms of content and structure. That common denominator turned out to be the Gospel of Mark. Of 660 plus verses in Mark more than 600 of these are found in Matthew and/or Luke. While Matthew and Luke each have their own individual outlines of Jesus' ministry, it is interesting that the two never agree together against Mark in points of structure and order. Matthew, and Luke also, may deviate from Mark's outline, but they never agree together in their deviation against Mark. These findings demonstrated that it is very likely that not only was Mark the oldest of the three but that Matthew and Luke had both used Mark as a source in the writing of their Gospels.

After removing the Markan materials from Matthew and Luke, one finds that there still remains, however, a large amount of material in both Matthew and Luke which did not originate from Mark's Gospel. Some of that material, composed mainly of Jesus' teachings, was to be found in both Matthew and Luke. It was then conjectured that a collection of Jesus' teachings had been compiled to preserve those teachings for the use of the early church. Some even suggested that the collection had been made at Antioch in Syria. Wherever it may have originated, this source became known as Q (for the German, *Quelle*, which means "source"). By understanding that Mark was used by the evangelists Matthew and Luke and that Q had been available to both these Gospel writers and also used by them, many scholars believed that the puzzle was solved with regard to the similarities among the three Gospels. The authors of both Matthew and Luke had used common sources, Mark and Q. This "two-document hypothesis" has been a very persistent element in Synoptic studies for many years.

Upon examining Matthew and Luke further, however, it becomes evident that much remains even after one strips away both the Markan and Q materials. Those blocks of material which remain usually reflect the special emphases of each of the two Gospel writers. At one point in the development of thinking about the Synoptic problem, it was suggested that the material special to Matthew (designated M) and the material special to Luke (designated L) had come from written sources. The solution to the entire Synoptic problem was then "solved" by what became known as the "four-document hypothesis." That scheme perhaps can best be diagramed to demonstrate how the Gospels came to appear in their present forms.

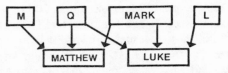

Further research into the problem of sources in the Synoptics, however, has led to some refinements in this schema. Some scholars have questioned whether Q or M or L ever existed as written documents. Most still believe that Q did, but there is real doubt today that either the M or L materials ever was written down in a single document. Most prefer presently to refer to M and L but understand these designations as simply convenient ways to specify the materials peculiar to Matthew and Luke. Some of M and L may have been written; some may have been oral. Again the interpreter is faced with a methodological discipline which can be very speculative in nature. But source analysis of the Synoptics is much more precise in some ways than form-critical analysis because one can (by the use of a *Gospel Parallels*) examine directly the materials under consideration. It is a good learning experience (and also fun) to take a *Gospel Parallels*, and by using different colors mark in one's own Bible the different sources to see for oneself why scholars have reached such conclusions about the sources used in these writings.

Redaction Criticism

As important and interesting as form and source criticism can be, it is nevertheless true that the real meaning of each Gospel can only be properly understood when each of these documents is used in its entirety, by itself, to learn how each particular evangelist interpreted the life and teachings of Jesus. Most persons, unfortunately, when studying the Gospels take bits and pieces from each of the Gospels to form their own portrait of the Founder of Christianity. While that kind of understanding may be meaningful to the person selecting the materials, what really emerges is a new portrait of Jesus which does not conform to any of the four inspired accounts. Correct interpretation of *these* documents is crucial to a person of faith, not some newly formed account! To interpret these accounts properly, therefore, it is imperative that each Gospel be studied individually and wholistically to determine the interpretation of Jesus that each evangelist has presented. Even among the scholars this was recognized, for after a long period of analytical investigation of the Gospels (with form and source criticism), a new approach came to be espoused in which each Gospel was studied as a wholistic unit. This discipline is known as *redaction criticism*.

It is by the method of redaction criticism that the beginning student should attempt to study the Gospels. This approach makes the assumption that each of the Gospel writers used different materials and traditions to weave together a portrait of Jesus. How the materials were used and edited in the early church has little relevance to the proper interpretation of these materials in the context of the Gospel itself. And further, it does not really matter from what source or type of source the material came. What matters is how the traditions were used by the Gospel writer to tell the story of Jesus of Nazareth, and that story is actually before the interpreter for study and examination. Therefore, to understand these four writings one must study each one separately to learn as much about its background and setting as possible so as to be able to understand the portrait of Jesus as depicted by each evangelist.

Mark

Since the Gospel of Mark was the first of these unique literary creations to be penned, it is best to begin with this work. Early in critical study scholars believed that Mark was the "least theological" of the four Gospels and that if one wanted to know Jesus "as he really was," one should study Mark. Gradually this idea had to be discounted, for as one studies Mark it becomes very clear that this is a highly theological document. (One is reminded also of the early tradition that Mark did not write his Gospel "in order.") To understand the particular emphases of Mark more clearly the interpreter must keep in mind that Mark was writing to the Christian community in Rome, which had just experienced a period of extreme persecution at the hands of Nero.

Mark writes his Gospel basically to depict Jesus as *the unique* Son of God. As the unique Son of God Jesus inaugurated a new kingdom and presented the guidelines for participation in that kingdom. It was a kingdom understood to be beyond the political institutions of this world and subject ultimately only to the One whose kingdom it is, namely God. In the role of unique Son of God Jesus is interpreted as the Messiah, but a different kind of Messiah from that which most Jewish people were expecting. He was to be a *suffering* Messiah, and Mark interprets Jesus' ministry against that kind of backdrop. This idea is presented quite clearly at the very beginning of Jesus' ministry, when after being baptized he hears a voice which says, "Thou art my beloved Son; with thee I am well pleased" (1:11). Here the reader or hearer of Mark's Gospel was to realize that this announcement from God substantiated the claim of the church that Jesus was God's Son. And just as important is the fact that it combines two passages from the Scripture, Psalm 2:7 and Isaiah 42:1. The first is from a "royal" psalm, sometimes interpreted as messianic, and the second is from one of the servant psalms of Isaiah 40—55. In other words Mark depicts Jesus as a suffering Messiah from the very beginning of his ministry. The point to be remembered is that Mark emphasizes the suffering of Jesus in a way that the other Gospel writers do not because this aspect of Jesus' life was so important to the people to whom Mark was writing.

This emphasis led to a closely related one, namely Mark's insistence that the disciples of Jesus were called upon to suffer also. It seems clear that this element was indeed a part of Jesus' instructions to the original disciples, but it is also clear that there is in Mark an inordinate stress upon that aspect of discipleship. The reason is obvious: that is the message the church in Rome needed to hear. Interestingly enough the disciples are depicted in Mark's Gospel as not ever really understanding why Jesus had to suffer or why they should have to suffer. This message would have struck a responsive note with the people in Rome also.

The last and most interesting, yet puzzling, aspect of Mark's presentation is the emphasis the interpreter finds upon secrecy. At first this element of secrecy was understood by interpreters to be connected with Jesus' messiahship. Some scholars suggested that this secrecy idea originated in the early church to explain why Jesus had not been recognized as Messiah by the Jewish people, an embarrassment to the early Christian community. On closer reading of Mark's account, however, it becomes obvious that the secrecy motif is not limited to one aspect of Jesus' person or ministry. At some points it appears that Jesus' messiahship is the issue in the secrecy, but at other points in the narrative it appears that different issues are involved, such as how Jesus healed or what Jesus did or what Jesus said. This complex problem is intensified by the fact that there are a few places in the Gospel where a direct command to "go tell" is made (cf. 5:19–20), and there are some teachings which specifically state that all things are supposed to be understood and made plain (cf. 4:21–25). This is a puzzling problem, indeed, and scholars have not as yet received a solution with which the majority of interpreters can agree.

Overall, however, Mark depicts Jesus as the bringer and proclaimer of the kingdom of God. Jesus is portrayed in this Gospel as one who acts, who is in constant conflict with the powers and forces of the kingdom of Satan. As God's unique Son and suffering Messiah, Jesus carries out his duty as it has been given to him as an obedient servant. Because of this obedience to God and God's kingdom, he has difficulties with people in positions of power and authority who misunderstand and abuse him, and who finally execute him upon a cross. All these motifs would have had great meaning to the people in the church at Rome, who were the recipients of this first Gospel.

Luke

The second Gospel to be written was probably the Gospel of Luke. This writing is unique among the Gospels in that it was written as the first volume of a two-volume work, Luke-Acts. The author of this work was probably the only Gentile Christian among the writers of the four Gospels, and his work seems to be more "general" in its orientation. After reading the prologues and the books themselves, the reader finds that this literary work appears to have been directed to a Roman official, "Theophilus," in particular, and to the Greco-Roman world in general. The reason for this can probably be located in the historical background of that period.

The Jewish people had been chafing under the yoke of Rome since about 63 B.C. when the Roman general, Pompey, conquered that part of the world for Rome. Among the many hopes of the Jewish people, there was a belief, widely held, that God was to intervene soon and remove the yoke of Rome (among other things). Certain people wanted this to occur so strongly that they began to advocate open war with Rome. Such persons were usually known as Zealots, and their thinking was that God would certainly intervene on their behalf in a war with Rome. Therefore, the sooner this war broke out, the sooner the yoke of Rome would be removed, and thus these patriots argued for open conflict with the Roman oppressors. Cooler heads prevailed for many years although extremists periodically gathered small bands of like-minded persons around themselves. Such persons were usually executed, and rather swiftly, by the Romans! In A.D. 66, however, a group of Zealots fanned the flames of hatred so much that the eagerly awaited war began. By September A.D. 70, the Romans breached the walls of Jerusalem, sacked and burned the city, and at least partially destroyed the temple. The Jewish revolt had been squelched.

This event held great historical significance both for the Jewish people and the early Christians. Up until this time the Christian movement had been by and large looked upon as a sect movement within Judaism. By about A.D. 70, however, the Christian church had grown and developed enough, especially in the larger Greco-Roman world, that it could be taken seriously as a separate entity. And further, after the 66–70 war between Rome and the Jewish people in Palestine, the Christians were anxious to dissociate themselves from the Jews so that they would not be identified with a group which had just fought a war with Rome.

This event also was important in that it appears fairly certain that many of the early Christians believed that when the temple was destroyed (Jesus had predicted the destruction of the temple cf. Mark 13:1–37), Jesus would return. (Whether this was what Jesus meant is not the issue here.) The temple had been destroyed, but the return of Jesus did not take place, not at least in the way the early Christians expected it to occur. After A.D. 70 Christians began to rethink the belief that Jesus would return soon. This idea had to be re-evaluated. Different ideas were espoused by different New Testament writers, and the three Gospels which were composed after A.D. 70 (Matthew, Luke, and John) all deal with the problem somewhat differently. Some scholars have even suggested that this one problem, the delay in Jesus' return, lay at the heart of Luke's reason for writing his two-volume work. That suggestion is probably greatly overstated, but there are elements in Luke's writing which appear to bear upon that problem. The most important reason for Luke's writing, which was conditioned by the destruction of Jerusalem and the temple, is probably the attempt (mentioned above) to dissociate the early Christian movement from Judaism.

The overall emphases of Luke's Gospel are more well known than those for Mark. Luke depicts Jesus, Messiah of the Jews, as the universal Savior of the entire world. *All* people were to be recipients of this "good news," especially the outcasts of society—the poor, the powerless, the despised (such as the Samaritans), even women! There is a decided appeal in this writing for people to be truly "pious" (in the best sense of that word), to understand the importance and significance of God's presence in all of life. As a corollary of this emphasis one finds prayer and the work of the Spirit central in the lives of those who have accepted the new life of the kingdom. Perhaps the most interesting motif which runs through both the Gospel and Acts is that which emphasizes the political innocence of Jesus, of the early Christian leaders, and of the Christian movement in general. It should be obvious from the brief historical discussion above why this motif is so prominent.

As one reads this Gospel, it becomes apparent how Luke has utilized the materials and traditions available to him to portray the significance of Jesus. For example, the announcement of Jesus' birth is made to Mary (not to Joseph as in the Gospel of Matthew). When Jesus is born, the angels tell poor shepherds working at their rather unsophisticated task. The heroes in this Gospel are Samaritans and poor wretches, even a rich tax collector (an outcast also) whose life is transformed. Further, in this Gospel Jesus is tried not only before Pilate but also before Herod Antipas, both of whom find that he is not guilty of any political wrongdoing. The centurion at the cross who had said in Mark, "Truly this man was the Son of God!" says in Luke, "Certainly this man was innocent." The resurrection stories take place in Judea and Jerusalem with the disciples instructed to wait in Jerusalem for the gift of the Spirit which was to be the triggering device for the spread of the good news to the world. (In Matthew and in Mark the resurrection appearances were to occur in Galilee—though if there were any of these in Mark, they were lost.)

Matthew

The Gospel of Matthew has always been one of the most popular of the Gospel accounts. Many persons who are not even "religious" are familiar with and attracted to the teachings of the Sermon on the Mount. This document probably emerged from somewhere in Palestine late in the first century, perhaps A.D. 80–100. It appears to have been written by a Christian who had formerly been a Jew, who wrote to similar persons in the midst of a larger Jewish culture and community. (Conflict between these two groups at times became rather vicious.) This explains the strong emphasis in this Gospel on Jesus as the fulfillment of "true Judaism."

There is little in Matthew's Gospel of a secrecy motif. Most (though not all) of Mark's secrecy passages have been purged of that idea. For example, Mark had interpreted the use of parables by Jesus as being for the purpose of hiding the message (cf. Mark 4:10–12). In Matthew's Gospel the same episode and quotation from the Scripture (Matt. 13:10–17) are interpreted in such a way as to place serious consequences upon any person who rejected the kingdom because its nature and importance had been made clear—by Jesus' use of parables! Another illustration of this point is evident in that the private experience of Jesus at his baptism (Mark 1:9–11, "Thou art my beloved Son") has been transformed into a public proclamation in Matthew's version (Matt. 3:16–27, "This is my beloved Son"). While there is still in Matthew's Gospel the motif of Jesus as suffering Messiah, this author is much more interested in depicting Jesus as the proclaimed King of (the new) Israel. At his birth rich, powerful people "from the east" came bearing gifts appropriate for a king. There is no mention of poor, outcast shepherds as in Luke.

Jesus as portrayed in this Gospel is a magnificent teacher as well as a king. The author has taken many teachings of Jesus which are found scattered throughout Mark and Q sayings scattered throughout Luke and added materials from M and structured these sayings together into "sermons." Many scholars claim that there are five of these sermon collections (cf. chaps. 5—7; 10; 13; 18; 24—25), and some have argued that this arrangement was done deliberately as a device to identify Jesus with Moses (cf. the five books of the Torah). Whether this is a legitimate interpretation of these collections (there may be more than five, cf. also chaps. 11 and 23) is still debated. It is true that this Gospel writer not only strongly depicts Jesus as the fulfillment of the true Judaism but also takes pains to identify him with as many of the Hebrew "greats" as possible, e.g., Abraham

(1:1–17), Moses, David, the prophets, etc. To illustrate this point more specifically, the evangelist quotes as often as possible from the Hebrew Scriptures to show how Jesus' life and teachings fulfilled those Scriptures. In most of these instances, however, the author does not understand the fulfillment in a literal predictive way, but understands fulfillment at the level of the deeper meaning of the texts (cf. especially Jesus' teachings about the law in 5:17ff.).

Several clues in Matthew's Gospel indicate that this is a later writing. There is the phrase "unto this day"; the church seems to have developed into a group wherein there are those who are deeply committed and those who are not; this Gospel is the only one in which the term "church" is used; and there is a decided emphasis on the delay in the return of Jesus.

This Gospel seems to have been designed for Christians who had formerly been Jews and who found themselves in the midst of a strong and sometimes hostile Jewish population. The number of quotations from Scripture which point to the truth of the Christian interpretation of the life and teaching of Jesus lend credence to the idea that the Gospel was to be used as an apologetic device in dealing with the Jewish community surrounding them. The collection of Jesus' teachings into blocks of material probably served as a teaching aid used for new Christians who had recently become converts, to give direction for living the new life of the kingdom.

John

The last of the Gospels, the Gospel of John, is very different in many respects from the Synoptics. Even though some of the stories and traditions about Jesus were obviously shared by the Synoptics and John, there is a decidedly different interpretation and usage of them in John's gospel. The early church fathers were also puzzled by these differences, and the "classic" explanation of this problem came from one of them, whose analysis was that John had written a "spiritual Gospel."

The critical problems (the who, what, where, when, why) connected with this writing are "legion." Examination of these issues is not the purpose of this study, but it must be pointed out that the content in the document itself has been presented in such a way as

to attempt very hard to associate the materials in this Gospel with
the Apostle John. These traditions may indeed be tracked back to
the Apostle John, but it is also clear that the traditions in John's
Gospel are very different from those found in the Synoptics. Even
when the traditions obviously refer to the same events and episodes,
they are interpreted and used very differently by the author of this
document. The question of the author's use of sources is not as evident in dealing with this Gospel as it is with the Synoptics. Some
scholars have suggested, however, that this author may have used a
"signs" source and perhaps a "discourse" source, but these ideas are
certainly not demonstrable beyond the shadow of a doubt.

Upon studying this Gospel, it is evident that the portrait of Jesus
depicted here is different from those presented in the Synoptic Gospels. In the Synoptics Jesus is the bringer and proclaimer of the
kingdom of God; in John's Gospel Jesus reveals God and speaks
about eternal life. In the Synoptics Jesus' teaching is done in typical
wisdom fashion by parables, pithy sayings, and hyperbole; in the
Fourth Gospel Jesus speaks in long involved discourses. In the Synoptics Jesus' ministry lasts only about six to twelve months; in John
it lasts almost three years. In the Synoptics Jesus goes to Jerusalem
only once, cleansing the temple on that lone visit. In John Jesus goes
to Jerusalem very often and cleanses the temple on the first visit. In
the Synoptics Jesus eats the Passover meal with the disciples on a
Thursday evening and is crucified on Friday, the day of the Passover;
in John Jesus eats a fellowship meal with the disciples on Thursday
evening and is crucified on Friday, the day before the Passover.

Certain familiar elements in the Synoptic presentation of Jesus
are missing in John's Gospel. There is no baptism of Jesus, only a
vague reference to it. There is no secrecy at all; Jesus is recognized
immediately by the disciples as the Messiah, the King of Israel.
Therefore there is no recognition scene, which was so important to
the Synoptic structure (cf. Mark 8:27–30 and parallels). There is no
agony in Gethsemane in John either. These are simply a few of the
differences.

To determine when this Gospel was written or for what purpose
or by whom is not an easy matter. There is a strong feeling that the
traditions included in this Gospel were in some way related to the

Apostle John. It is also clear from an examination of the material that several problems were being addressed in this document. There is a decided *antidocetic* motif incorporated into the story. Late in the first century under the influence of a certain type of Greek thought, the idea arose that Jesus was not really human, that he only "seemed" or "appeared" to be. The Greek word for "to seem" is *dokeô*, thus the term *docetic*. This Gospel emphasizes, therefore, that Jesus was indeed human (cf. especially 1:14). Another problem alluded to in the Gospel appears to be related to some antipathy between the Christian community and the Jewish community. There are strong indicators which point in that direction (cf. 8:39–59; 9:24–41; 19:1–16, to cite only a few). Specifics are not easy to find, however, and the simple truth is that very little is known about the origin of and circumstances surrounding the writing of this portrait of Jesus.

The primary purpose of this Gospel seems to have been to present Jesus as the true (i.e., authentic) giver of life and revealer of God to the world. "Life and light" are constantly recurring themes. There is a continuing summons in this Gospel for persons to have real, genuine "faith." This faith is not to be based on external signs but on an inward relationship with God and with Jesus, God's *Word*. To dramatize and emphasize that point, the Gospel appears to have been purposely written to present two levels of understanding—a superficial, crudely literalistic level and a deeper, spiritual level. For example, everyone misunderstands Jesus, his teachings and his actions, and these misunderstandings form the occasion for long discourses explaining the spiritual truth which the author intended the reader to learn and comprehend. The classic example of this is found in the Nicodemus story (chapter 3), but almost every account in the Gospel has in it some element of this method.

The author of this Gospel challenged the community to become truly a community of faith, faith not based on externals but on that inward relationship which could not be broken, not even by physical death (cf. 14:1–3). The climax of this teaching is to be found in Jesus' response to Thomas who had finally seen him after the resurrection, "Have you believed because you have seen me? Blessed are those who have not seen and yet believe" (20:29). The appeal of true religion is to have faith not based on external signs or props.

The richness of the four accounts of Jesus' ministry and teachings is evident. How unfortunate it has been that persons have failed to utilize these riches and have been content with bits and pieces pasted together to form a portrait of Jesus that is pale and uninspired.

Suggestions for Further Study

Achtemeier, Paul J. *Mark*. Philadelphia: Fortress Press, 1975. Proclamation Commentaries.

Briggs, Robert C. *Interpreting the New Testament Today*. Nashville: Abingdon Press, 1973.

Craddock, Fred B. *The Gospels*. Nashville: Abingdon Press, 1981. Interpreting Biblical Texts Series.

Hunter, A. M. *The Gospel According to John*. Cambridge: Cambridge University Press, 1965.

Kee, H. C. *Jesus in History: An Approach to the Study of the Gospels*. 2nd edition. N. Y.: Harcourt, Brace, Jovanovich, 1977.

Leaney, A. R. C. *A Commentary on the Gospel According to St. Luke*. 2nd edition. N. Y.: Harper & Row, 1966.

Martin, Ralph. *Mark: Evangelist and Theologian*. Grand Rapids, Mich.: Zondervan Publishing House, 1972.

Nickle, Keith F. *The Synoptic Gospels: Conflict and Consensus*. Atlanta: John Knox Press, 1980.

Schweizer, Eduard. *The Good News According to Mark*. Translated by Donald H. Madvig. Richmond: John Knox Press, 1970.

———. *The Good News According to Matthew*. Translated by David E. Green. Atlanta: John Knox Press, 1975.

———. *The Good News According to Luke*. Translated by David E. Green. Atlanta: John Knox Press, 1984.

Smith, D. Moody. *John*. Philadelphia: Fortress Press, 1976. Proclamation Commentaries.

VIII

How to Interpret Letters

Most of the New Testament writings apart from the Gospels, Acts, and Revelation fall into the general category of "letters." The writing of letters was a common practice in the Greco-Roman world. Usually a letter was addressed to a specific "occasion," i.e., written with regard to a particular situation. The letter had a standard form, and if the interpreter is aware of the structure of the letter, the individual components will be easier to identify. Usually the letter began with a *salutation* which identified the sender of the letter (and any persons with him) and the recipients of the letter, and included a greeting or a blessing. This was followed by a *thanksgiving*, usually to the gods, in gratitude for something special which had happened to or for the sender of the letter or the recipients or both. Then followed the *body* of the letter in which the primary reason for writing was discussed. This was all brought to an end with a *conclusion* which could contain personal greetings, travel plans, a blessing, or the like.

From this brief description, the interpreter will understand almost immediately that letters are even more historically based than other biblical writings. They were written to speak to specific circumstances, and this is true of the New Testament letters, especially those of Paul. For him the letter was the instrument by which he gave instruction, direction, and guidance to the early Christian communities founded during his journeys. Some scholars have argued that Paul considered these letters to be substitutes for his actual presence in the churches. In whatever manner Paul himself understood the letter, it is a fact that he wrote many and in them he attempted to speak to the needs and problems of those struggling communities. News about such needs and problems came to Paul's attention in two ways: (1) from letters written to him seeking advice on various issues; and (2) by word of mouth brought to him by persons in the churches or by his friends and fellow workers. Paul was, in the letters, speaking to specific problems and issues in the particular churches addressed.

That fact makes it both easier and more difficult to interpret his responses! In some instances the modern interpreter can determine rather precisely what the problem was, and that information can assist the interpreter to analyze the answer Paul gives. It is also true in other instances, however, that the modern interpreter has to make an educated guess as to the problem that Paul was addressing. No letter *to* Paul has survived, only Paul's responses. This is equivalent, as some have said, to listening to only one half of a telephone conversation! The situation is not as difficult as it may seem, however; for even though the questions may have been lost, the responses are usually clear enough so as to be properly understood even though the exact background for the answer cannot always be known.

Having said this, one must also be aware of a common misconception about and misunderstanding of Paul's teachings. Through the centuries of the history of the church, Paul has been frequently looked upon as "*the* Christian theologian," and when theologians want to write their "theologies," Paul is most frequently used for these enterprises. Whether this is legitimate is not the issue in this discussion. What is important for the interpreter of Paul's letters to keep in mind is that in these letters are specific answers to specific problems. The content is, therefore, much more practical than theoretical, more religious than theological. Paul himself was much more interested in Christian living and lifestyle—as were most of the New Testament letter writers—than he was in "proper and orthodox theology."

Another dimension to this problem should be mentioned at this point. Paul quite frequently, in responding to issues presented to him by the churches, would respond by using analogies or analogous-type arguments. Most persons today know what an analogy is and that it is a very misleading practice to attempt to make technical points of the various elements in the analogy. And further, it is just as misleading to push illustrations used as analogies to ridiculous extremes. One is reminded at this point of the misuse and literalization of Jesus' wisdom sayings. Unfortunately, however, far too many interpreters of Paul have never realized that he used such devices in his letters, and they have attempted to literalize and theologize comments which were originally intended only as figures of speech.

In attempting to understand letters, therefore, the interpreter must learn all that can be known about the historical circumstances surrounding the writing of the letter, learn all that can be known about the specific problems addressed in the letter, and understand something about the style of the letter writer, i.e., what methods were used by the writer to get across his points and ideas. In other words, what was the writer of the letter attempting to say to the people in the church(es) which was (were) being addressed? What problems were "solved," and what principles and guidelines were involved in these solutions presented to the church? Perhaps it would be most illustrative to examine one of Paul's letters briefly to demonstrate these points.

1 Corinthians

The letter of Paul which deals with the largest number of problems is 1 Corinthians. The church at Corinth was established in about A.D. 50 by Paul and his lieutenants in the midst of a very sordid society. Corinth was so well known for its immorality in the Greco-Roman world that a verb form was made from the noun Corinth which meant something like "to practice gross degeneracy." One can already anticipate that this church was probably not always going to be "proper," at least until the newly committed members learned just how different the Christian lifestyle was supposed to be from the one to which they were accustomed. The church in Corinth was quite active, if not always proper, and Paul's relationship with this church was at times very stormy. It is known from a close examination of the Corinthian letters that Paul wrote at least four letters to this church.

The first (mentioned in 1 Cor. 5:9) has been lost, and what is presently known as 1 Corinthians was probably the second letter Paul addressed to these people.

The letter known as 1 Corinthians resulted from Paul's hearing about a variety of problems which had emerged there. Some of these issues came to his attention in a letter written to him by someone(s) in the church (cf. 1 Cor. 7:1) while others came by word of mouth (cf. 1 Cor. 1:11 and perhaps 16:17). In this letter, therefore, Paul attempted to give answers to these various problems as best he could and in accordance with the principles of the Christian life as he understood them.

First of all, a problem with factionalism in the church basically revolved around the various leaders known to that church. Different groups within the church were championing the virtues of different leaders—Paul, Apollos, and Peter. Some were even claiming to be "of Christ." This latter group may have been related to a *Gnostic* thought pattern which was common in the Greek culture of that period. These people believed that salvation came through knowledge (*gnosis* in Greek means "knowledge," hence the name Gnostic), and they also believed that once they were in possession of this knowledge they were better than and different from ordinary people. Some scholars believe that those who claimed to be "of Christ" were Gnostic in their thinking. It is interesting to note that Paul devotes a great deal of space in chapters 1 and 2 to a discussion of real knowledge versus false knowledge. And in chapters 3 and 4 he argues that human leadership is a gift from God and should be accepted as such without regard to any exaltation of the leaders.

A second problem revolved around a man who was a member of the church living with his "father's wife," i.e., his stepmother (chap. 5). From Paul's comments it appears that the people of the church interpreted such behavior as acceptable in that it demonstrated the "new freedom" found in Christ. The lifestyle was not only accepted but in some sense applauded! Paul is aghast at such thinking and doing. He reminded the people in Corinth that even the Roman law did not tolerate such behavior and urged the people to ostracize this person from the Christian fellowship. (In that culture it was a far more serious matter to be ostracized from a group than it is in our society.) Paul believed that by denying this person membership in the Christian community two important consequences would or could occur. First, there was the matter of the witness of the church to the society in which it was situated. Paul understood that the church was not composed of sinless people and could never be at least in this world, but he also believed that the people of the Christian community were supposed to be radically different in lifestyle from the "people of the world." This difference was supposed to be observable by any who would take the time to look at the Christian community with any degree of objectivity. The purity of the church had to be safeguarded; *gross* immorality could not, therefore, be tolerated in one of its members.

The second consequence which Paul was hoping for with this type of action by the church was the ultimate restoration of the individual. Showing their displeasure at such activity and thus demonstrating the severity of the problem, the people of the church would be making clear to the offender just how far "out of line" he had strayed. And further, it would now become the responsibility once again of the church to do all it could to work with this person for his ultimate restoration to the new life in Christ (cf. 5:5).

Another problem addressed by Paul (6:1–8) was the ludicrous spectacle of Christians suing each other in the pagan law courts, not being able to settle even small matters of fairness, etc., among themselves. Paul again argues that such behavior does not demonstrate any positive witness to the outside world which may be looking at the church and how its members behave. He urged Christians to be fairminded and settle disputes between themselves.

Paul addresses two closely related problems at this point in the letter (6:9—7:40). Both of these are connected with Gnostic thinking. Some Gnostics believed that the created world and all its components were evil, so much so that people who had become "spiritual" were to have as little to do with the world as possible, even to the point of withdrawing from society to live some type of ascetic existence. Others believed that once persons became "spiritual," the old rules and regulations of the world were no longer binding or applicable for them. They could do anything they wanted to do, anywhere, anytime, with anybody. These two extremes are usually designated as "ascetic" and "libertine" or "antinomian" Gnostic ideology respectively. As already indicated, Gnostic thought patterns were brought by the people of the Greco-Roman world into the church with them. Paul and numerous other New Testament writers constantly had to be on the alert against the manifestations of these types of thinking and attempt to rid the church of the "perversions."

Sexual Morality

The first matter related to these ideologies (in 6:9—7:40) concerns the problem of certain men in the church frequenting "houses of ill-repute"—whether the cultic prostitutes of the religions of the city or the more common type is not clearly stated. Their rationale was quite simple: physical needs must be met, and physical matters are not important to a truly "spiritual" person—therefore, these "needs" may be met anywhere at anytime by anyone available. The mores and regulations of human society are no longer binding upon them. Paul argues from the standpoint of the Hebrew view of human makeup, that human beings are a single personality or entity resulting from the combination of a physical component and a spiritual component. It is not possible in Hebraic thinking to divide a human being into self-contained segments. The term Paul uses for the unity of human personality is "body." (He used the word with other connotations also, and this fact sometimes causes confusion among those who are attempting to understand his writings.) In 6:12–20 the term "body" seems to carry this nuance, however. Paul understands that human sexuality is more than simply physical acts. It involves the entire personality or being of a person. In practicing such activity (as Paul is arguing against here) much more is involved than the simple union of two physical bodies. The entire being of one person is merged with the essential being of another person. Thus if one is morally evil, the other is infected with that same evil, causing harm to the specific individual and any community with which that individual is associated—in this case the church.

The second problem Paul addresses here evolved from ascetic thinking which understood all (or at least most) physical activity as inherently evil. The problem was that people who were married were concerned about their sexual activities. If any physical dimension of life is tainted with evil, then should the Christian not abstain from everything that could be shunned, especially sexual relations? An additional problem lay in the area of couples who were about to be married. Should they marry or remain single and celibate? Paul's answer to these questions seems somewhat confused, especially if the interpreter does not study the entire passage in its context and against the backdrop of its own time.

From Paul's response it seems likely that some people were advocating sexual abstinence even within the bounds of marriage. Paul cautions them not to stay apart for a long period lest they be tempted to do something that would be detrimental to themselves and the church. His concession here to married couples then is that they could be allowed to abstain for a short period if both were agreeable. His advice to persons not already married was that they remain single. Some have argued from this that Paul viewed the unmarried life as "more holy" than the married life. If one looks closely at the text, however, one finds that this is not true. Paul believed, as did the entire early church, that Jesus was going to return soon, in their lifetime, and that preceding that return there would be a period of intense persecution directed against the people of God. Paul's advice here is practical, based on that understanding of the *Parousia* (Jesus' return). When intense persecution comes, it would be best to have as few responsibilities and encumbrances as possible; and one would certainly not want to have small children who would have to suffer in this period of trial and hardship. The answer Paul gives to the question of whether persons should marry is pragmatic not theoretical here. Attempts to make more of these teachings than Paul intended are violations of the text. One final note should be observed: Paul, in spite of his pragmatic opposition to marriage at this moment, nevertheless emphasized in several places that people who married were in no way sinning nor was their life somehow less "pure" than others who did not.

Liberty and Responsibility

The discussion in chapter 8 (extended in 9:1—11:1) is very interesting. A question had arisen in the Corinthian church concerning the matter of eating food which had previously been offered in sacrifice to a pagan god (i.e., an idol). The belief then was that some-how the god permeated the meat which the devotee ate, causing the god to become part of the worshiper. The person making the offering usually could not eat all of a sacrifice so that anything left over was sold by temple personnel to sustain the on-going work of that reli-gious group. It was very difficult in Corinth to avoid eating meat or food which had been offered to an idol. Some persons in the church were concerned that eating such food constituted an act of idolatry against Jesus and God. Others argued that such thinking was non-sense because there were no gods to enter the meat.

Paul's answer to this question is illuminating and also disquiet-ing. He agreed in theory with those who held that there were no gods and thus there was no idolatry in eating the meat. There is another aspect, however, which Paul considered more important than that. This question is not whether something is right or wrong in itself but rather whether one's action leads another person in the wrong direction so that that person is "destroyed." If such could possibly happen, Paul argues that the Christian must refrain from anything which could cause that situation to transpire. Here he placed a huge burden on the Corinthians and on subsequent generations of Christians. The followers of Christ are to place the genuine needs of others first, so that persons are not destroyed by the actions of "self-confident" Christians. Paul then wrestles with the problem of and tension between freedom and responsibility (9:1—11:1). In this seg-ment Paul uses the analogy of the athlete who exercises self-control, restraint, and discipline in training for the prize of victory. Accord-ing to his teaching Christians are to exercise self-control and disci-pline also in their daily lives.

Decorum in Worship

A series of problems dealing with proper decorum in worship forms the content of 11:2—14:40. The first item is the question of how women should be garbed when praying or preaching in church services. Interestingly enough the issue here has nothing to do with *whether* women can perform these assignments but rather with what is proper attire for them when they do. The specific cultural problem underlying this discussion is simply lost to us; several theories have been presented but no one of them has received universal acceptance. Whatever was at issue obviously stemmed from a cultural matter of that time and place. Paul argues here that women should have their heads covered when praying or preaching in church and uses a rabbinic type argument from Scripture to support his directive. Interestingly enough the text he chose went beyond what is really intended, and this caused him to insert a parenthetical statement which reinforces his own idea that women and men are equal (cf. 11:11–12).

A second item in this series results from the improper celebration of the eucharist (the Lord's Supper). In the early church it is probable that this celebration was done at a full-scale meal called an *agape*, a love feast. In the Corinthian church the more well-to-do were arriving early, eating up most of the food before others could arrive, and some drinking so much wine that they became drunk. Paul was not pleased at this behavior and instructed the Corinthians to celebrate this sacrament properly, in humility, and by "discerning the Lord's body," i.e., the church.

Another problem had two components: a general division among the people as to who had the most important "gift" to use in the life of the church, and a specific idea held by some that *glossolalia* (speaking in tongues) was the highest gift and should be practiced in all the worship gatherings of the church. Paul argued that all human talents are gifts of God and should be used for the "building up" of all the people of God, not for personal glory or gain. He uses the famous analogy comparing the members of the church to the members of a human body. Each has a function to perform; and if one of these is not functioning properly, the entire body suffers. All of these gifts or talents are to be used for the good of the church, and each must be used and evaluated by higher "gifts," in this case the gift of love. Paul argues in chapter 13 that no action can be "good" unless it originates from the proper motivation, namely genuine care and concern for God and other members of the community.

The discussion then narrows to the specific problem of glossolalia, an ecstatic type experience in which a person supposedly has been taken over by the Spirit and utters sounds that are unintelligible as a known language. These sounds were understood in that culture and time to be messages from God. When the experience was over, someone then had to interpret the message. As one can readily ascertain, there was a large opportunity here for persons to call attention to themselves and to enhance their own feelings of importance. Such activity had obviously reached such a level in Corinth that this type of behavior was disruptive to the worship services. Paul's advice here (14:13–33a) is for such activity to be curbed, especially in regular worship services where outsiders would probably be in attendance. He further understands that such activity could be controlled (14:28), something that many later advocates of the experience have argued against even though Paul certainly does assume this important dimension of the issue.

The Resurrection

Finally, Paul turned to discuss problems related to the issue of resurrection (chap. 15). The questions were: (1) was Jesus really raised? (2) will Christians really be raised? and (3) what does it mean to be raised; what kind of body does one have in the life which continues after this? The first question Paul put to rest rather simply. Jesus appeared to a large number of people, Paul included; if one doubts that Jesus was raised, go ask those who saw him since most are still alive. Paul then argues in a rather circular fashion to answer the second question. If Jesus was raised, Christians will be raised. If the dead are not raised, Jesus was not raised, but he was. Therefore resurrection is a real possibility for all those in the proper relationship with Christ.

The most interesting item in this discussion is the answer to the third question. What human being has not been curious about what happens after death? These Corinthians were also and asked Paul about the matter. The interpreter must beware in approaching these last verses lest current popular ideas impose themselves into the investigation of the meaning of this text (15:35–58). Paul is here attempting to explain something that he does not know about, at least first hand. He is not here attempting to paint a picture of heaven with specific details outlined for each part of the process of getting there and what will be seen and heard upon arrival. He is using an analogy again to speak to the specific concerns of the Corinthian Christians on this matter and to suggest understandable concepts about this mysterious experience called death, and the even more mysterious one revealed through the experience of Jesus called resurrection.

He uses the figure of a seed falling into the ground to describe analogously what happens in the resurrection for the people of God. (These are the only ones discussed here.) Paul indicates that a seed falls into the ground and dies; out of that occurrence comes a new life, a new plant, which in external form, at least, bears no resemblance to the seed. Implicit in this, however, is the idea that what emerges from the death of the seed is directly related to what the seed was. (One does not produce apple trees from peach pits!) All that is really implied is that just as human beings presently have bodies which are suited for life in a "physical" existence, they later will have bodies suited for life in a "spiritual" existence. It is in the spiritual realm that *the final victory of God* will be accomplished (15:50). Paul believed in that victory with all his heart.

Chapter 16 contains personal greetings, travel plans, and the like, and thus forms the conclusion to this rather lengthy discussion of problems in the church at Corinth. From this very brief examination of the background, issues, and Paul's responses, the interpreter already can see how important it is to understand the occasional nature of the letter style as exemplified in the New Testament. Each letter must be studied carefully to learn as much as one can about the background for the writing. If this is done, there is much greater likelihood that the document can be interpreted properly.

Authorship and Context

Space does not permit a detailed examination here of each of Paul's letters or of the others as well, but there are several matters related to letter writing which yet need to be mentioned. The first concerns the custom in that era of writing letters or books in the name of someone else, i.e., pseudonymous writing. Such a procedure was widespread in the world of that time and was not looked upon as immoral or illegal. It was simply part of the cultural milieu of that age, and it should not surprise the student of the biblical writings to learn that some of the biblical books are pseudonymous. This is especially true of the New Testament letters. Most of the letters which bear Paul's name are believed to have been written by Paul. Some, however, have been questioned, the major ones being 2 Thessalonians, Colossians, Ephesians, and the Pastoral Epistles (i.e., 1 and 2 Timothy and Titus). There is also question about the authorship of many of the others, i.e., 1 and 2 Peter, Jude, and James. Hebrews is an anonymous writing, though it has sometimes been attributed to Paul; and the Epistles of John identify the author as John the Elder, whoever that was. With the exception of Paul, very little is really known about the writers of most of the epistles.

A second consideration to which the interpreter of the letters must be alert is the fact that in addition to learning as much as one can about the specific "occasion" for the writing of the letter, the interpreter must also keep in mind that the letters may contain in themselves other types of literature. There were hymns in use in the early church, and some of these may have found their way into the letters. Most scholars are agreed, for example, that Paul used an existing hymn in his comments to the people in Philippi (cf. Phil. 2:6–11). Some also feel that a hymn may have been incorporated into the text of Colossians 1:15–20. Others find evidence of the use of liturgical pieces in Revelation (e.g., 4:8, 11; 11:17–18).

Some letters also appear to have been originally a homily or sermon. Such an interpretation has been made of 1 Peter 1:3—4:11. The argument is that this large portion of 1 Peter was originally a baptismal sermon delivered in the context of the worshiping community at the time of the baptism of new converts signifying their admission into the community of God's people. This sermon was then given a salutation and some concluding remarks and presented in literary form as a letter. Some scholars also feel that part of Colossians was a baptismal liturgy since there are several allusions to baptism in that letter.

The book of James has frequently been understood as a homily or at least a collection of wisdom-type teachings. Since most of these teachings are in exhortative style, some scholars have argued that James is a collection of *paraenetic* teachings (i.e., ethical exhortations). The book of Hebrews, likewise, is a difficult one to catalog or categorize. It does not have an epistolary salutation but does contain an epistolary type conclusion. Some interpreters have found in

Hebrews a Greek-type discourse and others a rabbinic-type discussion. Upon close examination it appears to be rather a combination writing exhibiting certain characteristics of each of several possible literary types. Hebrews does, however, like James, reflect a specific historical context and addresses problems which were being experienced among the people to whom the writing was originally directed.

Historical Setting

To understand the various letters contained in the New Testament, the interpreter must learn as much as possible about the historical setting for the writing of each particular letter. Such information may come from external sources, i.e., what the traditions say about the background for the writings, but the most helpful information for proper interpretation will probably emerge from a careful study of the writing itself, i.e., the internal evidence.

Many problems faced the early church during its formative years, especially in the postapostolic age, i.e., the period of time from 70 to 150. Problems dealing with the nature and work of Jesus, the mission and structure of the church, and the embarrassment over the failure of the Parousia to materialize as the early church had hoped dominate the writings of this period. With the exception of Paul's letters and the Gospel of Mark, almost all of the New Testament books were composed after 70. The primary consideration for the interpreter of the letters and "near" letters of the New Testament is to attempt first of all to understand the message for the church and its members as originally intended by the authors. Approaching these materials in this way is a safeguard to keep the modern interpreter from reading the documents as a twentieth-century rather than a first- or second-century person. Principles when gleaned in this way can then be applied to new and analogous situations today.

Suggestions for Further Study

Barrett, C. K. *A Commentary on the First Epistle to the Corinthians.* New York: Harper & Row, 1968.

————. *A Commentary on the Second Epistle to the Corinthians.* New York: Harper & Row, 1973.

————. *A Commentary on the Epistle to the Romans.* New York: Harper & Row, 1957.

————. *The Pastoral Epistles in the New English Bible.* Oxford: Clarendon Press, 1963.

Bruce, F. F. *Paul, Apostle of the Heart Set Free.* Grand Rapids, Mich.: Wm. B. Eerdman's Publishing Co., 1977.

Caird, G. B. *Paul's Letters from Prison: Ephesians, Philippians, Colossians, Philemon in The Revised Standard Version: Introduction and Commentary.* Oxford: Oxford University Press, 1976.

Cousar, Charles. *Galatians: A Bible Commentary for Teaching and Preaching.* INTERPRETATION. Atlanta: John Knox Press, 1982.

Efird, James M. *Christ, the Church, and the End: Studies in Colossians and Ephesians.* Valley Forge, Pa.: Judson Press, 1980.

Fitzmyer, Joseph. *Pauline Theology: A Brief Sketch.* Englewood Cliffs, N. J.: Prentice Hall, Inc., 1967.

Guthrie, Donald. *Galatians.* London: Thomas Nelson & Sons, 1969.

Houlden, James L. *A Commentary on the Johannine Epistles.* London: A. & C. Black, 1973.

Leaney, A. R. C. *The Letters of Peter and Jude.* Cambridge: Cambridge University Press, 1967.

IX

Conclusion

After the interpreter has deciphered what the text of the biblical writings meant originally, the question then becomes how that meaning—set as it is in the context of different historical circumstances, different cultures, different thought patterns, and presented by sometimes quite different literary types and genres—can be somehow transported to modern settings and still have relevance for contemporary society. In fact, some question whether the biblical writings can be made relevant to the contemporary world, whether these ideas and teachings, as interesting as they are, can ever be more than mere "curiosities" from the past. For the person who believes that the Bible is God's revelation to the world, the question is not *whether* these teachings are relevant but rather *how* can the application of these teachings be made in and to contemporary society and individual lives today. The assumption for such people is that these documents are more than mere literature or history from another time and place.

A Matter of Faith

To be sure, it is only by a "leap of faith" that a person can affirm that in these books one finds *the* revelation of God to the world, that the revelation can and does make a difference in people's lives and in the way they relate to God and to each other. Why should these writings be held in more esteem than the writings of anyone else? Many classical documents both ancient and modern have had dynamic impact on human civilization and individual lives—the philosophies of Plato or Aristotle or Zeno, the laws of Rome, the mystical writings of Hinduism or Buddhism, the wisdom of Confucius, to cite only a few. Why are the books of the Bible afforded a greater sanctity than these others? The answer has to be in the faith response of the communities which have been sustained and strengthened by devotion to the teachings of these documents and in the faith response of individual people who have claimed to have experienced the transforming power of God in their lives. Other strong arguments could be marshalled in defense of the intrinsic value of these writings, but the faith dimension is *the* one which must be basic. It is also an argument which cannot be either denied or authenticated by empirical evidence alone.

If one does affirm for oneself this faith dimension with regard to the biblical books, how then can one best apply the biblical teachings to present culture and society with its different thought patterns and complex technological problems? As has been argued throughout this book, the key to understanding the biblical writings and thus to understanding what and how to apply the teachings of these writings lies first of all in the discovery of what the biblical text originally said and meant. Contrary to some popular opinions, however, it is not then a matter of simply taking the text and imposing it "as is" on present problems in life and society. If the task is not so simple, can it be done? And if it can, how can one begin to learn to apply correctly the ancient biblical teachings in a modern setting? It is not an easy task at all but rather a task filled with uncertainties and ambiguities. To appreciate that point the reader may find it interesting that high level scholars have been involved in a great deal of discussion of late about the "hermeneutical" problem, i.e., the problem of the application of the biblical teachings to human existence in this time and place. While there is some agreement among those who are wrestling with the issue, no real consensus has as yet been reached.

The purpose of this book has not been to address the "hermeneutical" problem but rather to offer some guidelines and suggestions which will give direction to the person who wishes to interpret the Bible properly. The recurring theme of these chapters has been that one cannot apply biblical teachings to modern settings unless one knows first what the biblical writings meant originally. Perhaps a few suggestions for the difficult process of making a connection between the meaning then and the application now would be helpful and useful, however.

Principles

Contemporary persons who are sincere in wishing to take the Bible seriously for today's world must realize that there are in the biblical materials different types of teaching. Some passages, for example, seem to lay down principles as guidelines for proper living by anyone who wishes to be a part of God's community of faith. Secondly, other texts seem to lay down *specific commands* to be followed in every instance. Thirdly, certain teachings seem to be more directly related to specific historical events or occasions. Without taking those contexts into consideration, the teachings cannot be properly understood, and any principles or commands in such texts may seem to be rather arbitrary and rigid if absolutized into dogmatic legalisms. The proper understanding of each teaching appears to be directly related in most instances to the type of literature used to convey the instruction. Knowing such background, along with a healthy dose of common sense, will assist the interpreter greatly in the application process. Perhaps a few illustrations will demonstrate this point, which admittedly is somewhat elusive.

A study of 1 Corinthians has already been made, albeit rather superficially (cf. pp. 110–18). A number of problems had arisen to which Paul made answer in this letter as he felt appropriate. Paul's response to one of these problems in particular stands out as a good example of a principle which can be used as a guideline for living as a member of God's people. In 1 Corinthians 8 Paul argued that even though it was not immoral or wrong in any way, theoretically, to eat meat which had been offered to idols, there was a principle which transcends that "absolute" statement. This principle suggests and requires that Christians are to evaluate their actions not by some absolute standard that "anything not immoral can be done" but by an additional dimension which deals with how those actions influence and affect other persons. The principle or guideline which Paul espoused was that Christians should do nothing which would "destroy" a fellow human being, even if what they were doing was not in itself wrong or immoral.

This teaching by Paul is clear enough. Some may not really like what Paul says, but his directive leaves no real room for doubt. Modern persons, however, do not have a problem with food offered to idols, at least not in most western societies. The problem for the modern interpreter is whether the principle involved in this teaching has any real relevance for contemporary society. And if one believes that a positive response to that concern is appropriate, another question arises as to where, how, or when the teaching should be applied. Many considerations must be taken into account before one can simply "apply" the principle to some modern problem. What is the difference, for example, between simply "annoying" one's neighbor and "destroying" that neighbor? The conscientious interpreter is led into a consideration of modern society and present-day problems with regard to the "destruction" of a human being. Does Paul intend in his teaching only to imply a spiritual dimension within a person which is important and which can be destroyed "in the future"; or does he understand the destruction of a human life more broadly than that? Can this destruction take place in this life? If the latter was intended, then Paul's principle can be applied much more broadly. It raises the question of what in modern society can "destroy" someone? Alcohol, drugs, neglect, hunger, prejudice, injustice, etc.? How many of these could possibly be appropriately identified with Paul's principle? Another issue which broadens the discussion is: are certain elements which can destroy a person more specifically dealt with in other portions of the biblical materials? What is the teaching there about such issues? How far can one go in applying these ideas to specific issues in modern life?

One can readily surmise even from this brief discussion just how complex is the process of applying the ancient biblical principles to modern settings. The interpreter is forced to make some judgments about biblical principles, modern society, and contemporary behavior. How far can one principle be pushed without regard for principles and guidelines found in other biblical writings? Exactly where can that principle be applied appropriately in contemporary life? It seems logical that when one applies the teachings of the biblical texts to modern settings that there must be some type of *analogous situation or context* (either historical or psychological or whatever) into which the principles are placed. This would help to deter indiscriminate application of teachings in situations not really suited for the principles. It would further guard against arbitrary interpretations which only perpetuate "pet" theories of overzealous persons who attempt to read their own ideas into the biblical materials and then make inappropriate application of those ideas as if they were inspired revelation. The appeal here is for care and caution on the part of the interpreter; however, one should not become so cautious as to be immobilized in this endeavor.

Specific Commands

A second type of directive has to do with passages which seem to contain certain specific commands. The Ten Commandments could certainly be used as illustrative here. Just how far one should take specific commands, however, can also be debated. There is a commandment, for example, which states that a person is not to kill. The meaning of the text does not in its original setting exclude all killing because in those days killing in war or in self-defense or in the execution of someone for the commission of a capital crime was perfectly acceptable. The underlying idea here is the sacredness of life as a gift from God, so that any unnecessary and unwarranted destruction of life was to be avoided and was considered a violation of God's law. How far should a modern interpreter take this specific demand? Obviously one must consider not only the directive but the underlying meaning as well. This is clearly to be observed in Jesus' handling of the command in Matthew 5:21–26. How far can one go, therefore, in pushing this specific command? Is it too subject to other principles and guidelines? Is it legitimate to literalize the command from Exodus and Jesus' interpretation of it (given in a wisdom method incidentally) as a basis for pacificism or abolition of capital punishment, or opposition to abortion, or unilateral disarmament, or the like? Again one must ask what other types of teaching in the biblical materials must also be "factored in" when these more specific issues are debated. Even when specific commands are given, larger interpretative issues also must be considered.

Similar Settings

A third way in which biblical materials may be applied is by understanding that the teachings which emerged from specific historical settings must be applied in similar or analogous historical settings. For example, in Romans 13:1-7 Paul urged the Christians at Rome to be obedient to the "governing authorities," i.e., the state. This comment has been absolutized by some interpreters into a legalism; one must be obedient to the civil state no matter what. In the book of Revelation, however, the author pleaded with the Christians not to honor the state, to refuse to do what it asked them to do because of conscience and loyalty to Christ. Others have used this passage as an absolute teaching to urge disobedience to the state and even actual subversion to overthrow the state when they disagree with anything which the state does or proposes. Here is a case where personal "preferences" frequently take over, and the biblical texts are again abused by being cited as authoritative for human interpretations not in the texts.

How does one reconcile these two teachings about the state, however? How can they both be "true"? Here is a classic example of historical background and context assisting in the understanding of what is being taught. In regard to Paul's letter, the interpreter should remember that Paul wanted to come to Rome and to use that place as a base of operations for a missionary enterprise in the "West" (to Spain). Paul had been greatly assisted already in his work up to this time by the *Pax Romana*, the "Peace of Rome," which had been firmly established by this period of history. That area of the world had known wars and instability for literally hundreds of years, and the tranquility which Rome had finally brought was a welcome relief. Rome had also imposed its system of laws on the areas which it ruled and had developed a marvelous system of roads and communications. All these had been of great benefit to Paul's work and the emerging Christian church, and Paul believed that the benefits of that system were indeed a gift from God for both pagans and Christians alike.

Paul obviously knew that a Roman governmental official had given the final order for Jesus to be crucified. He himself had felt the injustice of corrupt officials who did not administer Roman law properly. In short, the Roman state was not the kingdom of God. Nevertheless, he obviously believed that there were more positive than negative elements to the rule of Rome at that time, more good generated than evil. Therefore he urged Christians as part of their Christian duty to support the state. There can be no progress in a state where chaos and anarchy exist.

The historical situation had changed when the author of Revelation wrote that book to people who were being persecuted by the Roman government. Domitian, the Roman emperor, wanted to be acknowledged as "Lord and God," and he demanded that the people in the province of Asia Minor give obeisance to him as emperor and to Roma, patron goddess of the Roman state. Christians refused to do this, believing that such would constitute an act of idolatry. Because of this refusal they were persecuted, and Rome became for them the incarnation of evil. The author of Revelation, therefore, urged the Christian people not to honor the emperor or the state because it was demanding a devotion from them that they could only dedicate to God. The resistance urged was not described as armed subversion or aggressive disobedience but rather as the continued witness to the one true God by refusal to perform acts of worship for the state or the emperor.

How can these two conflicting teachings about the relationship of a believer to the civil authorities be used as a guideline for people in today's world? Few emperors are left, especially in western society, and governments can be changed by voting privileges granted to citizens. How do these teachings direct the modern interpreter in relating to the state? Where is the line between a state which generates more "good" than "evil" and the state which is more "evil" than "good"? The principles set forth in these passages need to be supplemented perhaps by further directives from other parts of the Scriptures and from the use of one's mind and heart as these are led by the same Spirit of Truth which inspired the ancient writers. Another element can also be utilized in this process. Many of the biblical writers seemed to use it, but it is often a rare commodity in modern society, namely the element of common sense. Some of Jesus' parables and Paul's teachings assume this "uncommon" commodity in dealing with many of the difficult problems of life. Guidelines there are in abundance in the biblical writings; specific absolute commandments are few and far between. This makes the task of the person who wishes to correlate the biblical teachings with present life difficult, challenging, and fascinating. After all the hard work necessary to understand the biblical texts in their historical settings, common sense can help in the process of application.

This discussion has focused on how one should go about interpreting the biblical text itself. Only a few guidelines have been given here for the task of reapplication or *hermeneutics*. Two basic principles seem to be *sine qua non* for this task, however. First, the biblical text must be understood in its original meaning and setting insofar as that is recoverable. The second guideline must be that between the original teaching and setting and the present setting there must be a similar or analogous set of circumstances into which the old principles will fit. One question which could be asked is this: if present day religious thinking and action supposedly based on the biblical accounts were to be used as standards for interpretation, would the principles and guidelines from these settings fit back into the old biblical settings and still maintain the same standards and ideas as the originals? If so, perhaps one may be on the right track in this tedious and difficult process.

Conclusion

There is no need to prolong the discussion of this point. The purpose of this book has been to give guidelines for proper understanding and interpretation of the biblical writings. Several comments are perhaps appropriate in the light of the total discussion. First of all, it is exceedingly clear that the old "proof-text" approach to the interpretation and application of the biblical texts cannot be tolerated any longer. This approach has produced weird interpretations of the text, weird applications of the text, and even weirder theology. It has led to aberrations of behavior and produced extremely dangerous situations both in individual personal lives and in the larger arena of human history.

Secondly, no matter what method of approach one may find most congenial (cf. chap. I), it is a matter of extreme importance for the interpretation of the Bible that the text be allowed to speak for itself and not be used to support personal ideas and principles which are simply not in the text. If one wants to believe, for example, that the world is going to come to an end in such and such a year and that certain modern nations are going to be involved in that event, etc., that is one's right. It is not one's right, however, to impose those ideas on biblical texts which have no relationship with such thinking. Let the Bible speak for itself; let these documents say what was originally intended. It is the task of the true biblical interpreter to discover what the writings said and meant originally even if that interpreter does not agree with what the text says! What is needed today is a basic understanding of what the Bible is and some direction as to how one can go about beginning to learn to interpret the biblical writings correctly. One cannot know how to apply the teachings until one knows what the teachings are!

The task of learning how to interpret the Bible is not an easy one, but it is certainly not impossible nor out of the reach of lay persons who sometimes despair at what appear to be technicalities beyond their understanding. If a person leaves the interpretation of the Bible solely to others, then that person can never really know if the interpretations being presented are correct and the applications being made are in line with what the text really means. If a person really wishes to learn how to interpret the Bible properly, he or she can do it. The task will not be easy nor will the time required to do the job right be short. The results, however, will be more than worth the effort, for it is in the pages of these writings that God is revealed to the world.

Additional Suggestions
for Further Study

To become a serious student of the Bible, the beginner should become acquainted with certain basic resource books for use in continuing the quest to become a faithful interpreter of the Bible. The following books are recommended from a large list of materials available. No attempt is made to list all the available sources, not even all the good ones. These have been chosen because they will be of significant assistance to the beginner. The reader is also reminded of the lists cited at the conclusion of each chapter.

Bible Atlas:

Oxford Bible Atlas. H. G. May, ed. New York: Oxford University Press, 1962.

Bible Dictionaries:

Dictionary of the Bible. James Hastings, ed. Rev. ed. by F. G. Grant and H. H. Rowley. New York: Charles Scribner's Sons, 1963.

Harper's Bible Dictionary. Madeleine S. Miller and J. Lane Miller, eds. 8th rev. ed. New York: Harper & Row, 1973.
    This dictionary is especially helpful to the beginning student and a completely new edition is scheduled to appear in the near future.

Interpreter's Dictionary of the Bible. G. A. Buttrick, et al., eds. 4 vols. Nashville: Abingdon, 1962. Supp. Vol., 1976.

One-Volume Bible Commentary:

The Interpreter's One-Volume Commentary on the Bible. Charles M. Laymon, ed. Nashville: Abingdon, 1971.

Histories of the Times:

John Bright. *A History of Israel.* Third ed. Philadelphia: Westminster Press, 1981.

F. F. Bruce. *New Testament History.* Rev. ed. London: Oliphants, 1971.

Historical-Critical Introductions to the Old and New Testaments:

B. W. Anderson. *Understanding the Old Testament.* Third ed. Englewood Cliffs, N. J.: Prentice-Hall, Inc., 1975.

James M. Efird. *The New Testament Writings: History, Literature, and Interpretation.* Atlanta: John Knox, 1980.

————. *The Old Testament Writings: History, Literature, and Interpretation.* Atlanta: John Knox, 1982.

Robert A. Spivey and D. Moody Smith. *Anatomy of the New Testament.* Third edition. New York: Macmillan Co., 1982.